Digital Wisdom

Digital Wisdom

Leading Transformation with the Sophia Factor

Alfonso Asensio

BEP

BUSINESS EXPERT PRESS

Leader in applied, concise business books

Digital Wisdom:
Leading Transformation with the Sophia Factor

Cover design by Cassandra Kronstedt

Interior design by S4Carlisle Publishing Services, Chennai, India

First published in 2025 by
Business Expert Press, LLC
222 East 46th Street, New York, NY 10017
www.businessexpertpress.com

ISBN-13: 9-781-63742-886-3 (paperback)
ISBN-13: 978-1-63742-887-0 (e-book)

Big Data, Business Analytics, and Smart
Technology Collection

First edition: 2025

10 9 8 7 6 5 4 3 2 1

EU SAFETY REPRESENTATIVE
Mare Nostrum Group B.V.
Mauritskade 21D
1091 GC Amsterdam
The Netherlands
gpsr@mare-nostrum.co.uk

Description

This book is not just a roadmap for digital transformation—it is a manifesto for responsible innovation. It challenges leaders to think critically, act ethically, and stay adaptable in an unpredictable digital landscape.
—David Jones, Founder and CEO, The Brandtech Group

In an age of relentless technical change and disruption, is your organization struggling to adapt and stay relevant? True transformation demands more than technology; it requires wisdom.

Digital Wisdom: Leading Transformation with the Sophia Factor introduces a revolutionary framework that blends ancient philosophical insights with cutting-edge business strategies to help leaders navigate digital change with clarity and purpose.

Drawing on the classical concept of "Sophia" (wisdom), which encompasses understanding, sound judgment, and practical intelligence, this book examines contemporary challenges such as online identity, truth in the information age, and the nature of digital reality. It provides decision makers with the strategic foresight to lead with confidence and drive sustainable innovation.

Whether you're a business leader, consultant, or strategist, *Digital Wisdom* offers a blueprint for harnessing timeless insights from philosophers like Socrates, Plato, and Aristotle to elevate digital leadership. Discover how to cultivate companywide resilience, empower teams, and foster a transformative mindset that transcends fleeting trends, enabling your organization to thrive in the digital age.

Contents

List of Figures

Foreword

We are living in the most transformative period of human history. The digital revolution has changed every aspect of our personal and professional lives, redefining how we communicate, work, and interact with the world. And, it is causing a tectonic disruption in marketing—there is nothing that humans are currently doing that cannot be done better, faster, and cheaper with AI.

Yet, despite the incredible power of technology, businesses and leaders often struggle to harness its potential effectively. This book, *Digital Wisdom*, provides a timely and essential guide for navigating this era, blending modern technological strategy with ancient philosophical insights.

As someone who has spent my career at the intersection of technology, marketing, and business transformation, I have seen firsthand the immense opportunities and challenges that digitalization, and now AI, bring. When we launched The Brandtech Group, our mission was to help businesses adapt to a world where brands must move at the speed of digital. Today, whether you are a startup, a Fortune 500 company, or a creative entrepreneur, understanding the digital landscape is no longer optional—it is imperative.

What sets this book apart is its unique approach: Rather than focusing solely on the technical aspects of digital transformation, Alfonso draws on the wisdom of the past to make sense of our digital future. The book takes us on a journey through Heraclitus' ever-changing world, Aristotle's rhetorical strategies, and Socrates's method of critical inquiry, showing how these timeless principles can guide organizations through the complexities of the digital age.

One of the most interesting lessons in this book is the idea of Sophia (wisdom) as a guiding force in digital transformation. In an era where data is abundant but meaning is scarce, businesses must go beyond mere digitization and embrace digital wisdom—a philosophy that prioritizes ethical decision making, user-centric design, and sustainable growth.

In today's hyperconnected world, companies that succeed are those that put people at the heart of technology. The most successful brands of the future will be the ones that build trust; create meaningful experiences; and use AI, data, and digital tools to empower rather than exploit.

This book is not just a roadmap for digital transformation—it is a manifesto for responsible innovation. It challenges leaders to think critically, act ethically, and stay adaptable in an unpredictable digital landscape. Whether you are a CEO navigating disruption, a marketer crafting digital strategies, or an entrepreneur looking to scale your vision, *Digital Wisdom* offers invaluable insights that will reshape the way you think about technology and business.

As Alfonso brilliantly illustrates, the lessons of the past are more relevant than ever. And in an age of rapid change, wisdom—not just knowledge—will be the key to building a future that benefits both businesses and society as a whole.

—David Jones
Founder and CEO, The Brandtech Group

Preface: Why This Book

A few years back, I was in a Tokyo meeting room with a client.

The client's team was part of a large Japanese corporation looking to leverage digital technology to revamp its business and gain a competitive advantage. And they were in a good place for that; they had the resources, the human talent, the urgency. But as the meeting went on, I saw some worrying signs. They had not shared any specific example or compelling reason why the company needed to go through this very complex and expensive process.

Eventually, I asked what the objective was: Why did they want to "be digital" and where did they want to go as a company?

The team leader, after a moment, began to deliver a list of technical jargon: "AI-driven customer engagement," "blockchain-enabled supply chain," "data-optimized performance." He spoke with the confidence of someone reciting a memorized script, but he lacked any spark of genuine understanding. It felt as if they were chasing the latest digital trends without grasping the underlying principles or considering the human impact. They were attempting to build a digital future on a foundation of buzzwords, mistaking technical proficiency for true knowledge.

The room's atmosphere shifted and then I realized what the issue was: They were drowning in data yet starved of wisdom.

What they were missing was "Sophia."

Sophia (from which the term "philosophy" stems) is the ancient Greek word for "wisdom" but it is more than that; it embodies understanding, sound judgment, and practical intelligence. This book exists to argue that Sophia provides a crucial framework for navigating the contemporary challenges of online identity, truth in the information age, and the very nature of digital reality.

Digital Wisdom: Leading Transformation with the Sophia Factor is a book about digital transformation, not merely as a technical undertaking but as a human endeavor guided by the wisdom of Greek philosophy. It aims to illuminate the complexities of the digital world—its technologies, industries, and actors—through the lens of Sophia.

While modern issues like misinformation, social media addiction, or job displacement are amplified by technology, many of them are fundamentally human questions, echoing the inquiries of philosophers like Socrates, Plato, and Aristotle.

This book seeks to equip today's business leaders with the necessary wisdom to confront digital disruption with integrity and foresight by:

- Demystifying the complexity of the digital landscape.
- Offering practical guidance for digital transformation.
- Fostering a human-centered approach to technology.

By using Sophia and the lesson of classic Greek philosophy, we can advance toward a sustainable digital future guided by wisdom and navigate the modern age with clarity and purpose.

CHAPTER 1

Sophia, the Eclipse, and the Need for Digital Wisdom

The Battle of the Eclipse and the Love of Wisdom

Let me start this book, which is about digital technologies, online platforms, and the need for wisdom, by telling you a story about an ancient battle.

The battle was fought in the early sixth century BC by two armies at the River Halys in Anatolia (modern-day Turkey). Herodotus, the Greek historian often referred to as "The Father of History," describes it like this in his Histories, a lengthy account of the conflicts that took place between the Greek and the Persian people in the fifth century BC:

> War broke out between the Lydians and the Medes, and continued for five years, with various success. In the course of it, the Medes gained many victories over the Lydians, and the Lydians also gained many victories over the Medes.

The origins of the conflict are rather gruesome. According to Greek sources, the king of the Medes insulted some hunters when they returned to him with nothing in hand, so they retaliated by murdering one of the king's sons and feeding him to the Medes. The hunters took refuge in the Lydian capital and so began the war.

> Another combat took place in the sixth year, in the course of which, just as the battle was growing warm, day was on a sudden changed into night. This event had been foretold by Thales, the Milesian, who forewarned the Ionians of it, fixing for it the very year in which it actually took place. The Medes and Lydians, when they observed the

change, ceased fighting, and were alike anxious to have terms of peace agreed on.

It must have been terrifying for those soldiers, being in the middle of a violent encounter and suddenly, having the day turn into night. Even for those familiar with the idea of daytime eclipses, it may have felt otherworldly, supernatural. Were the gods angry at them? Was that the end of the world?

But, if you read that again, the most interesting section of the extract is in the last paragraph; not everyone was surprised by the phenomena. It says that a man called Thales from Miletus had predicted the eclipse. Thales is a famous figure, a thinker of the pre-Socratic era, often considered the first true philosopher of the Greek tradition. Thales was an iconoclast who brought forth a radical new way of thought. Rather than attribute real-world events to supernatural intervention, he is credited with examining naturally occurring phenomena via critical thinking. This was a radical shift from the existing orthodoxy that used theology to explain the world and a change that ushered in the enlightened tradition of scientific thinking.

Just as Herodotus is the "Father of History," Thales is the father of deductive reasoning.

It is debatable if Thales really predicted the eclipse. Most likely he didn't, and the prediction was ascribed to him by a popular opinion that Herodotus picked up in his book, but it makes for a good story. It fits the historical figure as we know it, so it may not be all that relevant if it indeed happened. The episode's significance, as American writer Isaac Asimov noted, was that the prediction of the eclipse marked the "birth of science." Before that time, all orthodox thought adhered to conventions that followed hereditary knowledge received from previous generations. Thales showed a way to understand the world that was groundbreaking in its approach, one that would later be known as the "Love of Wisdom."

Love Sophia, and Sophia Will Love You Back

Herodotus and Thales were not isolated cases. What we know as Classical Greece, the period of ancient Greek history that spans roughly from the fifth to fourth centuries BC, (specifically from the defeat of the Persian invasion in 480 BC to the rise of Alexander the Great in 323 BC) birthed a culture where thinkers strived to find specific and demonstrable answers to the mysteries of the cosmos. Classical Greece is the cradle of Western philosophical thought, and the very term "philosophy" conveyed the aspirational human search for knowledge and the pursuit of truth.

"Philosophy" can be translated as "Love of Wisdom" where wisdom or *Sophia* (Σοφία in the original Greek) as we will refer to it moving forward, means both practical knowledge for living well and profound insight into the understanding of things. It is important to emphasize that classical philosophy was not conceived as an armchair tool to ponder abstract and obscure concepts but as a search for answers to the absolute and vital questions troubling Greek thinkers: What is the true nature of the world and what place does mankind occupy on it? So, when the classical Greek philosophers started to inquire into the essence of reality, they had to resort to a novel way of reflection to find answers. The rational and systematic thinking process was born.

The year 585 BC is the accepted beginning of the philosophical tradition in the Western world. That is the year that Herodotus attributes to Thales of Miletus the prediction that stopped the war between the Medes and the Lydians. But as heavyweights like Socrates (469 to 399 BC), Plato (427 to 347 BC), and Aristotle (384 to 322 BC) broke into the scene and philosophy developed, Sophia transformed into a multifaceted concept. For Socrates, it was a tool for ethical self-discovery; for Plato, a pathway to transcendent truth; and for Aristotle, the ultimate intellectual endeavor.

Socrates: A Guide to Seek Knowledge and Question Assumptions

Socrates redefined Sophia as a map of the limits of knowledge and used it in the Socratic method he developed to propel ethical and intellectual inquiry. He believed that by questioning assumptions and examining life, individuals could uncover moral truths and live virtuously.

In a period where "received wisdom" (referring to the traditional beliefs, customs, and understandings passed down from previous generations) stifled active intellectual development, Socrates shook the foundations of learning by emphasizing critical inquiry over passive acceptance.

Sophia for him was an active, ongoing pursuit rather than a fixed state of knowledge.

Plato: The Path to Eternal Truths

A student of Socrates, Plato elevated the concept of Sophia by linking it to the pursuit of the Forms (eternal, unchanging realities like truth, beauty, and goodness that exist beyond the material world). In his work *Republic*, Plato described the philosopher-king as the epitome of a wisdom-oriented regent, capable of perceiving these higher truths and guiding society accordingly. For Plato, Sophia was not just intellectual insight but a transformative understanding that connected the soul to the divine order of the universe: a bridge between the temporal and the eternal, the physical and the metaphysical.

Aristotle: Practical and Theoretical Knowledge

Aristotle, a student of Plato, added a more systematic approach to the concept of Sophia by distinguishing between two types:

- Practical wisdom (*phronesis*): The ability to make sound decisions in daily life, particularly in moral and social contexts. He considered this type of wisdom as essential for virtuous living and good governance.
- Theoretical wisdom (*sophia*): A higher form of knowledge concerning the first causes and principles of existence. For Aristotle, this involved understanding the fundamental truths about the natural and metaphysical worlds.

Aristotle emphasized the importance of cultivating both types to achieve a balanced and fulfilling life, with Sophia being the crown jewel of human understanding.

Sophia 2.0

But surely, the understanding of people and the world that Greek philosophers held 2,500 years ago cannot have much relation with our modern reality of digital devices, personal data and online media platforms. What could be the link between that agricultural society which hugged the shores of the Mediterranean Sea, a place where the *polis* (or city-state) was the most complex social and political structure people knew of and our digital sphere, a globe-spanning cultural construct that dominates the world and has propped TikTok, Uber Eats, and the Amazon marketplace to the top of the mind and the front of the screens of that 66 percent of the global population (5.3 billion people) which has online access?

The answer? More than we may think at first glance.

As digital technologies, social media, cloud computing, and platform-based ecosystems reshape society, our understanding of wisdom, modern wisdom, has evolved to mean something different from the classical term. Because of our current needs, there has been a pivot to empirical knowledge so modern conceptions of wisdom often prioritize knowledge gained through scientific inquiry. Wisdom means for us the ability to apply knowledge effectively in real-world situations. It is focused on problem-solving and is domain specific. We value measurable knowledge, data-driven knowledge, and mercantile knowledge that is task and revenue oriented.

But this modern wisdom of the digital age seems to be failing to provide something essential: a reference frame in which to understand reality and our place in it like Sophia did for the Greek thinkers.

As inhabitants of the digital world, we can become confused about what is real and what is not. Think about the case of Justine Sacco, a former senior director of corporate communications who, in 2013, was at the center of a digital media storm when she posted a very controversial tweet to her 200 Twitter followers before boarding an 11-hour flight. By the time she landed, the post had gone viral and had been read by millions of people. The digital sphere was so enraged that her company terminated her contract. Or about the case of GameStop, a struggling videogame retailer, which in 2021 saw its stock price unexpectedly and sharply rise (from under $3 to as high as $483 in late January 2021), causing the hedge funds that had bet against it to lose billions of dollars. The increase didn't reflect the real value of the company but was the result of a concerted effort by online denizens (led by a single trader and live streamer) to upset the stock market.

Reputation and stock prices. Employment and wealth.

Actions in the digital world may be made of binary code, long strings of 1s and 0s, but have consequences in the real world.

In the current digital age, identifying what constitutes the real nature of the world may not be an easy thing to do. Are the relationships that we establish on social networks like Meta or LinkedIn less real than those with the people we meet in person every day? Are the scores a player achieves in a multiplayer online game less commendable than the goals scored in a friendly football Sunday match? Or what about money? Bitcoin is a virtual digital currency, but is it any less virtual than the money we move from our savings account when swapping a credit card to pay for dinner?

Digitalization, the transformation of work processes leveraging digital technologies, has dazzled our understanding of reality because, for most of human history, the essence of things was tangible and concrete. Leaving aside theological concepts of the supernatural, the world was what humans could see and touch. A coin was a physical coin, a book was a physical book. We can probably now agree that tangibility is not a requirement for reality anymore.

And this is where the principles of Greek philosophy and the digital sphere overlap, where the lessons of Socrates, Plato, Aristotle, and other classical philosophers become crucial. Their complex system of thought was rooted in "wisdom as Sophia" and offers a valuable lens for navigating our fast-paced technological world and addressing the challenges posed by this new digital reality.

Sophia and Information

Information may be knowledge, but it certainly does not confer wisdom on its own. In my professional career in the digital field, I have worked with many companies that, out of fear of missing out, hoard vast amounts of data that sit untouched in expensive databases. Without a critical look and a process to generate insights, all that data does is consume energy and, even worse, generate a false sense of accomplishment. For individuals, information was once a scarce commodity but has become so commonplace that it has lost most of its nominal value. We can access every detail about the fall of the Roman Empire and generative AI can produce a thousand-word report on the topic in a few seconds, but often all that wealth of data just flows from device to device, from person to person via forwarded links and videos, without being ingested and processed.

In many ways, the information superabundance we are living in has similarities with the caloric superabundance that is behind the obesity problem in the developed world. The Industrial Revolution of the nineteenth century transformed food production (both in farming and animal husbandry), so for the first time in human history, caloric scarcity was replaced with overabundance in vast areas of the planet. Wired as we are by evolution, living among vast amounts of food without clean lifestyle habits has had a tremendous impact on our physical health. Similarly, we are starting to see the effects that information superabundance that is not guided by a critical thinking process is having in the form of bias, echo chambers, and misinformation.

While we have access to more knowledge than ever before, information alone is not wisdom. Wisdom requires discernment; understanding which information is valuable, accurate, and ethically sound.

Sophia and the Ethical Use of Technology

Digitalization is not only about having data tools and information readily available at our fingertips and digital wisdom isn't just about knowledge or technical expertise. Companies and individuals have gained immense power of insight and behavior prediction by leveraging data, computing power and analytics engines. Traditional notions of Sophia apply nowadays as they emphasize ethical responsibility and thoughtful decision making when using that power.

Consider your favorite social media platforms. It is a marvel to see the unprecedented level of connectivity it enables and how that can help your personal and professional life. But think about the negative parts of it, the thoughtless comments, the aggressive behavior, the misinformation, privacy breaches, and mental health concerns.

A modern form of Sophia can and should provide tech leaders and users alike a sense of balance between innovation and moral foresight.

Not considering the long-term societal impact of our digital journey has created most of the problems we can find online today.

Sophia and the Idea of Human-Centric Technology

Individual users hold a contradictory position in the digital world. We are certainly the main beneficiaries of technological developments; all those tools allow us to book a flight online, speak to our friends and family at no cost from around the world and access scarce products and services to have them delivered to our doorstep. But we are also susceptible to being exploited by that same technology; our data is modeled, sold, and purchased by third parties, and our opinions can be manipulated by rogue players and groups of interest. In a world where data is the fuel of the whole system, users are the key ingredient; we are both source and destination, both the alpha and the omega. As the old adage goes, if you don't know what the product is, you might be it.

Sophia, in the digital context, can be a tool to emphasize a human-centered design for the whole technology sphere that enhances human well-being rather than the exploitation of users as commodities. Innovation that is balanced with empathy and understanding of the human condition is not a naïve concept but a way to ensure that digital solutions, from social media algorithms to cloud technology, serve a greater role.

We may be too late to erase some of the damage done by the wisdomless application of digital technology in some areas but at this stage of development, the ethical design of new systems in AI and machine learning algorithms is attainable. All that is required is some deep consideration of how they impact society and how they may perpetuate existing biases so fairness can be guaranteed.

Sophia as a Guide to Navigating Complexity

Technology, even the user-friendly one, can be overwhelming. Who here has not scratched their head when faced with a new consumer interface or when having to install and navigate a new app? What about that seething frustration of having to rely on an app to access your bank account or your concert ticket and finding yourself locked out of it and, no matter what you try, cannot log in?

While digital literacy increases daily and we are all much savvier now on the ways of the Internet and smartphones than 5 years ago, the complexity of the digital sphere sometimes surpasses its convenience.

Sophia in the modern world is about managing its complexities. The sheer volume of information, the speed of technological change, and the interconnectedness of systems require human wisdom to discern meaningful patterns, predict trends, and make sound decisions.

Sophia and Social Awareness

I remember the initial years of the user-accessible Internet. It is difficult to describe to digital native young people the wonder of the late 1990s and early 2000s when you could find information online. It was as if the walls of all the world's libraries, bookshops, and record stores had come crashing down courtesy of the digital information revolution and their content was floating freely in the digital ether for the taking. And the purest expression of that original spirit may still be Wikipedia. The still active reference website is a free resource built by open contribution and edited by a dedicated group of volunteers. Wikipedia has survived the upheaval of the many dot-com crashes and rebirths, and has challenged the expanding and often ruthless monetization patterns that have taken over the digital sphere.

Wikipedia is, in many aspects, the heir of the original inspiration for building the Internet as a space for scientific information exchange where social awareness and digital citizenship could be fostered. While the power of platforms like Meta (formerly Facebook), X (formerly Twitter), and TikTok to shape public opinion and culture often defaults to whatever reinforces their economic model, the potential for social collaboration that Wikipedia carries the torch for is still there. Discretionary wisdom is key to emphasizing the responsibility of content creators, platform owners, and users to promote truthful, respectful, and meaningful engagement.

Sophia in the classical Greek world called for the need to add ethical reflection to the communication process to prevent the dominance of authoritarian or religious dogma. In the digital space, it means reflecting on how digital tools affect democracy, privacy, and the mental well-being of society.

Sophia as a Method of Empowerment

Digital transformation is still unevenly distributed around the world. While developed economies enjoy advanced connectivity speeds and well-developed platforms, other regions like sub-Saharan Africa, areas in Central Asia, rural Latin America, and some Pacific Island nations lag behind. And even within the same economy, some groups may be left behind due to lower income levels, education gaps, age, and so on.

In this sense, Sophia embodies the idea of using digital tools to foster collective intelligence and open access to education, empowering more people to contribute meaningfully to society.

We know that access to digital capabilities is closely tied to economic progress, so it makes sense that true wisdom in our digital age means sharing that knowledge and those capabilities with everyone. We're all part of a giant classroom, sharing ideas and building on each other's knowledge, and Sophia can foster a kind of collective intelligence, where everyone has the chance to contribute something meaningful to society. It's about empowering individuals, not just a select few, to participate and shape our future.

Not Just Wisdom, but Digital Wisdom

All of that is to say that the objective of writing this book is aimed in three directions:

1. To explore the digital world and explain the different actors, technologies, and industries that are part of it.
2. To provide a practical, accessible guide to digital transformation, demystifying its technical complexities and offering clear, actionable strategies for companies and organizations seeking to leverage its power to achieve their strategic objectives.
3. To do all that not just through a functional prism but through a human one—a prism of sensible thought so that we can make sense

of where we are and where we are going and create a sustainable digital future both for individuals and enterprises.

And for that, I believe the concept of wisdom as Sophia, as well as many other lessons from classical Greek philosophy, is an invaluable tool. Despite all the trappings of modern technology and social change, we are, at our core, the same humans who grappled with fundamental questions about ourselves and the world 2,500 years ago. We share the same uncertainties but also the same competencies for curiosity and understanding.

We are heirs to the thinkers who looked at the sky during a spring day, saw the sun darken, and, amid the confusion, didn't just succumb to fear but instead asked, "Why is this happening?" and then set out to find the answer to that and to many other questions about the world and themselves.

CHAPTER 2

Heraclitus and the Changing Digital World

A Fast-Moving Digital Universe

The digital world is confusing.

It's fast-paced. It's changeable. It's a manic place. And the love it has for acronyms (DSP, SSP, IoT, DMP, CTR, CPC, API, GDPR, UI, SEO, UX, AI, etc.) makes everything even more perplexing.

At the corporate level, new companies offering complex services appear every day. Many overlap, are redundant, or release nonrelevant products that add to the noise. For existing and established players, there is a similar frenzy, with tremendous pressure to stay relevant and out of fear of missing out.

At the individual level, consumers get caught up in the whirlwind too. How many times have you changed your e-mail server (if you still use e-mail at all) since you first had access to the Internet? Older users of the service may remember AOL as the first dominant e-mail provider, then came Hotmail, and later Yahoo! Mail. Nowadays, Gmail and Outlook dominate the industry but who knows for how long.

How about social media? Have you found yourself spending time in different online spaces lately? Or maybe you've switched to some new apps that are just easier or better than the ones you used before? Anything you've discovered recently (a great trip planner, a super-efficient scheduler, or a fantastic translator) that's become your new go-to?

Users of digital technology, be it individuals or organizations, find it difficult to stay constant because services change or fade away, technology evolves, and what was so very useful a while back is suddenly obsolete. The digital world is quite changeable and that is a built-in feature because innovation is what keeps the industry moving ahead.

But there is a drawback. Companies looking to harness the power of digital technology to transform their business have a hard time distinguishing among the vast offer of vendors and providers or selecting what tech or tool they need to invest in. And for casual users who are not very technology savvy, having to adapt to a new phone, to a new app, or a new design takes time and effort. For example, we all know that new AI tools can increase personal and professional productivity tremendously, but investing to learn how to use them effectively is not always easy.

So, before we start discussing the digital sphere and the nature of digital transformation, there are three things we could do to reduce the complexity of the topic.

- Define what digitalization/digital transformation is.
- Learn how we got here and how the digital revolution has changed the world.
- Map out the digitalization/digital transformation process.

Many Sides of One Coin: Digitization, Digitalization, and Digital Transformation

Does turning something "digital" make it "better"?

We often hear about the magic of "going digital," and it's easy to assume that anything digital is automatically better. Just look at the impact of digital giants like Apple and Google, they've revolutionized how we live and work. The tech world has been buzzing about digital solutions for years, making it seem like everything that can be digital should be changed to make it digital.

But before we jump on the bandwagon, it's worth taking a closer look at what "digital change" actually means. There are three terms we can use when discussing the process of becoming "digital" and they are not exactly the same, even though they are sometimes used interchangeably.

1. Digitization.
2. Digitalization.
3. Digital transformation.

Digitization is the first one.

It refers to the conversion of analog information into digital form. For instance, scanning a document (converting handwritten notes into a PDF file) or creating a digital inventory of products and services. Digitization is the initial, basic stage but a necessary one. For information to enter the digital sphere, first it must be transformed into the correct format. If you go to see a new doctor for the first time, you may be asked to input your information into a digital device; name, address, and any ailments you feel. But maybe the clinic is not that sophisticated, and you are handed a sheet of paper to write it all down. The doctor can check your details there and then but unless there is an additional step where somebody pushes that data into a computer, a tablet or a similar device, it won't do much good. Next time you visit, the personnel at the clinic may have to shuffle through an archive of papers to find you instead of conjuring your data with the click of a button. Digitization helps by increasing productivity and efficiency while decreasing costs, but it is quite limited as a change because it focuses on information alone without changing the overall work process.

Digitalization goes a step further.

This is the process of leveraging a digital asset, like data, to optimize existing work processes and create value. Digitalization involves uploading that scanned document to a shared platform where people can collaborate in real time, thus improving operational efficiency. The first step of digitization just tackles the data format, but digitalization adds significant value. If the clinic you visited takes the accumulated data from all its patients, runs an analysis of the most common ailments, and figures out that a scheduled flu shot may reduce patients becoming seriously ill by half, that is a significant operational improvement. Digitalization, in this case, has resulted in value.

Digital transformation transcends both digitization and digitalization.

This is a broader, more strategic initiative that involves reimagining business models, processes, and even the company's culture through the integration of advanced digital technologies. The jump from digitalization to digital transformation is significant. When the online homestay marketplace Airbnb launched its services, it connected hosts offering accommodations or experiences with travelers seeking unique stays or activities. The platform leveraged a peer-to-peer model which bypassed the traditional hotel room booking hospitality model. Airbnb did not digitalize the hospitality sector by moving data from an analog format into a digital one (hotel operators had been doing that for years already), what the company did was digitally transform the industry by creating its Airbnb platform. The resulting revenue-producing and value-producing opportunities have changed the way people travel ever since. That is why true digital transformation isn't just about upgrading technology, it's about leveraging these innovations to create new sources of revenue related to a competitive advantage.

While the definition of digitization is commonly agreed upon, there are arguments to see digitalization as a wider process, one that includes many (or all) of the characteristics of digital transformation. Both terms are used interchangeably in many cases. This book will not be too strict in the distinction since both digitalization and digital transformation can be defined as this:

Digitalization, or digital transformation, is the process of reinventing business models through the integration of digital technologies. This involves not only technology changes but also the cultural shift, organizational restructuring, and strategic planning necessary to fully harness the potential of such technologies.

Nothing to See Here; Just Another World-Changing Revolution

One of the problems with writing about the transformation of the digital world is that we are neck-deep in it, and getting perspective can be difficult. Is this the biggest shift in human behavioral patterns we have ever seen? Has digital technology changed the way we see ourselves and the world? Or can we not escape the buzz and see the new social and economic digital reality as so significant because it's happening to us?

Digitalization is undeniably one of the most transcendent developments of our time, permeating nearly every facet of modern life. The integration of digital technologies has fundamentally altered how organizations operate, engage with customers, and deliver value. However, it's worth considering the historical context of this transformation. How does digitalization compare to other pivotal revolutions (such as the agricultural, printing, and industrial revolutions) that have driven profound societal shifts throughout history? Each of these earlier revolutions dramatically reshaped societal structures and economic growth, so how does the current digital revolution fit within this historical pattern?

The Agricultural Revolution

The Agricultural Revolution is often considered the most fundamental transformation in human history, as it allowed humans to transition from a nomadic, hunter-gatherer lifestyle to settled agricultural communities. This shift, which began around 10,000 BC, had far-reaching effects on nearly every aspect of life:

- Sedentarism meant cities. Before the Agricultural Revolution, humans relied on hunting animals and foraging for plants for their sustenance. This lifestyle required small, mobile groups that could move frequently to follow food sources. The development of agriculture and husbandry allowed people to domesticate plants and animals, leading to the establishment of permanent settlements. This transition was the foundation for the growth of villages, towns, and, eventually, cities.
- Cities meant complex societies. The development of farming techniques and the cultivation of grains like wheat and rice allowed for the production of surplus food. This surplus enabled populations to grow and laid the groundwork for more complex societies. Instead of existing in a constant state of survival, groups that generated additional food volumes could free up some of their members to become specialized operators. Religion, government, art, manufacturing, and warfare professionals became such because of readily available food stocks and social stratification.
- Societies meant culture and art. With the development of larger and more complex social structures, communication became paramount. Written systems were developed and, with them,

centralized governments, legal codes, and trade systems sprouted. But so did literature, structured religion, pottery, weaving, and other crafts.

The Print Revolution

The Print Revolution, sparked by Johannes Gutenberg's invention of the movable-type printing press around 1440, was a pivotal moment in human history. The spread of printed materials fundamentally transformed knowledge dissemination, communication, and societal structures:

- Democratization of knowledge: Before the printing press, writing material was a rarity, and books were manually produced items and therefore expensive. The printing press drastically lowered the cost of creating books and documents, allowing knowledge to spread more widely among the population. As a result, education and literacy expanded.
- Spread of literacy: As books became more affordable, literacy rates began to rise, particularly in Europe. With more people able to access written materials, new ideas moved faster. The rise of literacy empowered the general public to engage with literature, science, politics, and religion in new ways.
- Acceleration of innovation: The printing press played a critical role in accelerating the dissemination of scientific knowledge. The work of scientists like Nicolaus Copernicus and Galileo Galilei, which challenged the prevailing geocentric model of the universe, was spread more quickly because of printed books. The printing press also facilitated the expansion of Isaac Newton's groundbreaking discoveries in physics and mathematics, which were shared across Europe, fueling the Scientific Revolution.
- Cultural and religious impact: One of the most significant impacts of the Print Revolution was its role in the Protestant Reformation. Martin Luther's *Ninety-five Theses*, which criticized the Catholic Church, were quickly printed and distributed across Europe, giving rise to a religious movement that profoundly altered

society in the continent. The print medium also fostered the creation of newspapers and pamphlets, helping to shape public opinion and political movements over the centuries.

- Political and social change: With the wider distribution of printed materials, people became more aware of political and social issues. Ideas that challenged the status quo were widely circulated and inspired social movements and uprisings. The Enlightenment thinkers, such as Voltaire and John Locke, who emphasized reason, individual rights, and freedom of thought, were able to reach a much larger audience through print.

The Industrial Revolution

The Industrial Revolution, which began in the late eighteenth century in Britain, marked the shift from manual labor and agrarian economies to industrialized and mechanized production. This period fundamentally transformed the global economy and had widespread social, economic, and technological effects.

- Mechanization and automation: The hallmark of the Industrial Revolution was the mechanization of manufacturing. The invention of machines such as the spinning jenny, steam engine, and power loom enabled factories to produce goods at unprecedented speeds.
- Mass production: The introduction of the assembly line, most notably by Henry Ford in the early twentieth century, allowed for the mass production of goods. Products could now be made more quickly, efficiently, and at a lower cost. This change not only increased the availability of consumer goods but also laid the foundation for modern consumerism, resulting in increased demand and economic development.
- Urbanization: As factories sprung up, people moved from rural areas to cities in search of work. This led to rapid urbanization and the growth of major industrial centers.
- Rise of capitalism and economic growth: The Industrial Revolution laid the groundwork for the modern capitalist economy.

Wealth creation became linked to industrial production, and the pursuit of profit fueled innovation.

- Societal transformation: The Industrial Revolution drastically altered social structures. The rise of the working class and the accumulation of wealth in the hands of a few led to significant social and political changes, including labor movements, child labor reforms, and the eventual push for universal suffrage.

And Now, the Digital Revolution

As disparate as they may seem, the three cases above have something in common: they resulted from a set of circumstances that pushed scarce goods over the subsistence level. During the Agricultural Revolution, food was the main item, during the Print Revolution, information, and in the Industrial Revolution, manufactured products. As a result, each transformed the social, economic, and cultural outlook of the world.

But what about the Digital Revolution? Can we say with confidence that it has brought a similar change, not just to our present lives but to future generations?

The digital world, which began in the mid-twentieth century and continues growing today, is characterized by the rise of computers, the Internet, and, most importantly, data as a central asset. The shift from analog to digital technology has radically transformed every industry and created entirely new ways of communicating, conducting business, and organizing society.

- The rise of computers and the Internet: Early computers, developed in the 1940s and 1950s, were massive, expensive machines used primarily for government and military purposes. However, with advances in technology, computers became smaller, more powerful, and more affordable. By the 1980s and 1990s, personal computers entered homes and businesses, changing how people worked, learned, and communicated. The Internet, which began as a project to connect research institutions, became publicly available in the 1990s, leading to a global communication revolution.

- Data as a key asset: Data, much like oil during the Industrial Revolution, has become a critical resource in the digital age. Every digital interaction, whether a Google search, an online purchase, or a social media post, generates data that can be used to gain insights, improve services, and develop new products. Companies like Meta, Google, and Amazon have built entire business models around collecting, leveraging, and monetizing data.
- Automation and AI: Just as machines revolutionized production during the Industrial Revolution, automation and artificial intelligence (AI) are reshaping industries today. In manufacturing, AI-powered robots are performing tasks faster and more accurately than humans. In health care, AI is being used to analyze medical data, detect diseases early, and recommend treatments. Self-driving cars, digital personal assistants (like Siri and Alexa), and smart homes are all part of this wave of AI-driven automation.
- E-commerce and digital businesses: The Digital Revolution has also reshaped commerce. Online platforms such as Amazon, Alibaba, and eBay have become dominant players in global retail, allowing consumers to purchase goods from anywhere in the world. The rise of the "gig economy," powered by platforms like Uber, Airbnb, and Fiverr, has created new ways for people to work and participate in the economic boom but has also raised questions about the quality of employment and working conditions of the industry.
- Global connectivity: The Internet has connected people across the globe in unprecedented ways. Social media platforms (Facebook, X, Instagram, etc.) allow users to communicate, share content, and group together. Events like the Arab Spring and the rise of grassroots political movements have shown how digital platforms can be powerful tools for social and political action.
- Innovation and new industries: The Digital Revolution has spawned entirely new industries and business models. The app economy, for example, didn't exist before smartphones became mainstream. Today, app development is a multibillion-dollar industry that powers everything from food delivery to finance.

Similarly, the rise of cloud computing has transformed how companies manage their IT infrastructure, allowing them to scale quickly and reduce costs.

So, if each of the previous revolutions has been marked by technological advances that fundamentally reshaped society, the economy, and the way humans live and work, then the same can be said of the digital one. It has modified the human experience to a degree that makes it rank beside the other three.

Still, there seems to be something missing.

If this is indeed the momentous revolution that the future was all about, where are then the flying cars? Where are the weekends on the moon? Where are the androids serving our every whim? While life in the twenty-first century differs from the twentieth century, it does not seem to have ushered in a radically new lifestyle. Two primary reasons explain this discrepancy.

One is that this was an *expected revolution*. Hunter-gatherer groups were not waiting for someone to crack the farming techniques that would change their lives. Fifteenth century Europe did not watch with bated breath for somebody to develop a moving printing press and the people who saw the first clunky steam engine working at a coal mine in Tipton, England, did not figure that would change the world. But society at large was waiting for a future-proof change from about the middle of the twentieth century coinciding with the development of the atomic age.

The other reason is that it was a *counterintuitive revolution*. Although it was expected, it took a form that surprised the world. All the speculative thinking, scientific forecasting and science fiction fantasies we had, did not quite come to be realized. In exchange, we got things even more fantastic: music players that put "a thousand songs in our pockets," digital books that contain a full library, computers that fit in our hands and are 100,000 times more powerful than the ones used in the Apollo 11 lunar landing. That is because the Digital Revolution has not been an energy-powered revolution but a *data-powered* one.

Energy is still a scarce resource; we cannot keep cars flying or rockets running at a significantly lower cost than we did before. But data… Data is the fuel that powers the revolution because it is created constantly and leveraged just as fast to bring value. Data, which was originally a by-product of the digitalization process, is now the one factor that differentiates the digital age from the ones that came before. As businesses and organizations collect massive amounts of data, they gain the ability to make more informed decisions, enhance customer interactions, and improve internal processes, which in turn generates more data.

The Digital Revolution builds on the foundation laid by the previous three instances. It creates new dynamics that are driven, not by known essential staples like food, knowledge and energy, but by a new factor that we have created and learned to exploit, man-made lists of ones and zeros forming binary code.

Data: The beating heart of a data-driven revolution for a data-driven life.

The Digital Transformation Process: Asking the Right Question

So, if digitalization is so complex, where does a company looking at transforming itself or an organization that needs to incorporate digital capabilities start, particularly if it doesn't have a strong technological DNA? In a case like that, "Where do I start?" may not be the right question to ask.

Here is an interesting example of how asking the right question can make the digital transformation process much smoother. Blockbuster, once the world leader in video rentals, is infamous for its spectacular failure to adapt to the digital age. Netflix, on the other hand, is a company that started as a DVD mailing service (hardly a pedigree that screams "digital know-how") but managed to fully embrace digital streaming and, in the process, transformed the entertainment industry. Today, Netflix is a household name, while Blockbuster is a fading memory.

In retrospect, Blockbuster could have jumped into its digital transformation process by asking "Where do I start?" or "What technology should I adopt first?" They didn't, but even if they had, it would not have been the right question.

The question that the company failed to ask was one of *identity*: "Who are we and where are we going?"

Blockbuster was dominant in the videotape and DVD rental business (a business that developments in connectivity speed and digital streaming were already rendering obsolete in the early 2000s) and with good reason. They were a successful company with a large network of brick-and-mortar stores, their employees were mostly customer-facing store clerks and had perfected a work model centered on developing offline customer loyalty and repeated store visits.

But that was just the format in which they delivered their core service. Netflix had a much smaller and less store-dependent DVD mailing service and because of that, they understood that sending packages via mail was just one of the ways they could deliver movies and TV programs. Once the technology was robust enough to allow online streaming, they switched formats.

And here is the difference, Blockbuster failed to realize that they were not in the *videotape rental business* at stores but in the *entertainment* business, which happened to be delivered via that specific media format.

Every organization's journey toward digital transformation is unique, but asking the right questions early on will help identify where the need for change is coming from. Once that is answered, there are three additional questions the organization needs to address to define the digital transformation process.

- What are the drivers? What is pushing the organization to embark on digital transformation?
- What are the opportunities? What is there to gain if the company successfully transform digitally?
- What are the challenges? What is the risk if the organization does not transform?

What Are the Drivers?

Market competition: Sometimes you change not because you want to but because you have to. As digital technologies rapidly advance, companies must innovate to keep up with competitors and those who fail, risk being outpaced as was the case with Blockbuster.

Customer expectations: Modern customers are demanding. In the digital age, they (by which I mean, us) expect seamless, personalized, and convenient experiences across multiple channels. If you have tried the services of customer-obsessed companies like Amazon, which uses data on user behavior to make accurateproduct suggestions, you would be reluctant to downgrade.

Technology advancements: Emerging technologies such as artificial intelligence (AI), cloud computing, and the Internet of Things (IoT) are creating new opportunities for businesses to innovate. IoT, for example, gives the capability to monitor the performance of devices in real time, reducing downtime and enabling predictive maintenance for manufacturers.

Business agility: In today's fast-moving market, agility is critical. Businesses must be able to respond quickly to changes in consumer demand, technological advances, and global events. Zara, the fast-fashion retailer, has built its success on this agility. The company uses real-time data from stores to ingest customer feedback and adjust production, ensuring it always has the latest trends on its shelves. This responsiveness is a direct result of its digital transformation strategy, which integrates data into every part of the supply chain.

Cost efficiency: Digital transformation often leads to significant cost savings because it automates repetitive tasks and reduces operational inefficiencies. Walmart is a key retailer that has doubled down on this driver and has implemented automation in its warehouses, using robots to handle inventory and streamline logistics. The move has cut labor costs and has also improved the accuracy and speed of its supply chain operations.

Data-driven insights: Companies that can effectively harness data gain a significant competitive advantage. Starbucks uses its mobile app and rewards program to collect data on customer preferences. By analyzing this data, Starbucks can tailor its promotions to precise customer segments, boosting engagement and driving sales.

What Are the Opportunities?

Enhanced customer experience: Digital technologies enable businesses to provide more personalized and engaging customer experiences. Disney's MagicBand allows guests to access hotel rooms, purchase food, and reserve ride times; not only does this make the stay more convenient for the user, but the data that Disney collects, in turn, serves to improve its operations.

Operational efficiency: Automation and process optimization can lead to significant improvements in productivity and cost savings. Amazon, with its highly automated warehouses, uses robotics to deliver packages to customers faster than most competitors.

Innovation: Digital transformation fosters a culture of innovation, enabling businesses to experiment with new products, services, and business models. Tesla, for instance, is not just a car company, it's a technology company that works simultaneously with electric vehicles, autonomous driving, and clean energy solutions.

Data monetization: Many companies have turned their data into valuable assets. Google, through its advertising business, collects vast amounts of user data and monetizes it by selling targeted ads. This data-driven business model has made Google one of the most profitable companies in the world.

Agility and scalability: Cloud computing allows businesses to scale rapidly and adapt to changing market conditions. A company like Netflix, which streams content to millions of users worldwide, could not do that without a cloud infrastructure and the ability to quickly scale up its capacity during peak times, such as when releasing a new show, and scale it down during slower periods.

Ecosystem collaboration: Digital transformation thrives when there are opportunities for collaboration across industries and ecosystems. Apple has created an entire digital universe through its App Store, a central hub that allows developers to build applications that generate revenue while enhancing the functionality of Apple's devices.

What Are the Challenges?

Legacy systems: Technology can be expensive so many companies still operate with outdated IT systems, which make it difficult to integrate new digital technologies. And because technology influences the organization, those legacies affect business as well. Kodak was once a leader in the photography industry but struggled with this challenge. While the company invented the digital camera, its inability to shift away from its legacy film technology and business model marked its decline. In contrast, Fujifilm, Kodak's main competitor, embraced digital technologies and successfully transformed into a global imaging and health care company.

Cybersecurity risks: As companies digitize more of their operations, they expose themselves to greater cybersecurity threats. Equifax, a U.S. credit reporting agency, had done everything right during its transformation into digital, but the centralization of data and the use of web applications are what made it vulnerable to a data breach that in 2017 exposed the personal information of over 145 million people.

Skills gap: Talent is scarce when it comes to digital transformation and many organizations struggle to find employees with the necessary skills to implement and manage new technologies. McKinsey, a consulting firm, estimates that 87 percent of companies have skill gaps or will have one within the next few years.

Change management: Resistance to change is a major barrier to digital transformation. Procter & Gamble (P&G) encountered internal resistance when it embarked on its digital transformation journey. To overcome this, the company doubled down in culture-building and employee engagement, helping people understand how digital transformation would benefit both them and the organization.

Data privacy concerns: The Wild West days of the digital industry are over and stricter regulations such as the General Data Protection Regulation (GDPR) in Europe and the California Consumer Privacy Act (CCPA) in the United States require organizations to handle customer data with care. But challenges remain and companies must strike a balance between leveraging customer data for business insights and ensuring compliance with these laws.

Heraclitus, *Panta Rhei*, and the Changeable Nature of the Digital World

We started this chapter by talking about how confusing the digital world may seem, but we now have some key elements to make our approach more accessible:

- The subject: We have precise definitions of digitalization and the digital transformation process.
- The context: We have seen the historical impact of the digital revolution, giving us perspective on how we arrived at this point.
- The path forward: We have a structured guide to the digital transformation process, offering a practical starting point for change (Figure 2.1).

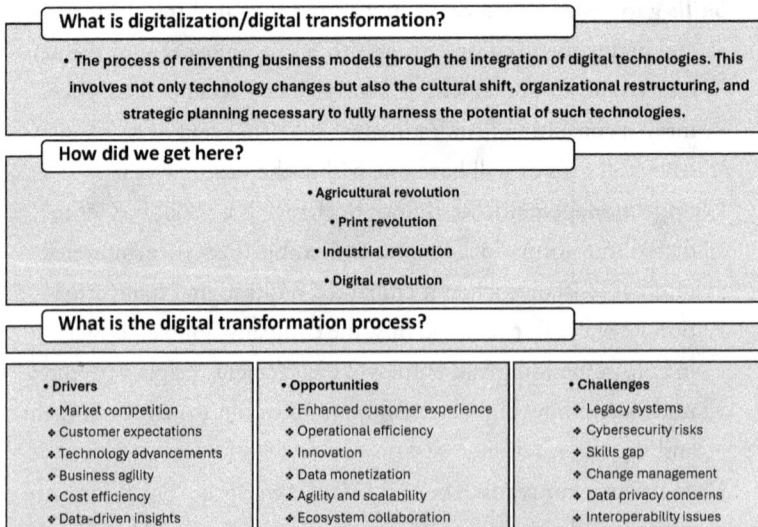

What is digitalization/digital transformation?

- The process of reinventing business models through the integration of digital technologies. This involves not only technology changes but also the cultural shift, organizational restructuring, and strategic planning necessary to fully harness the potential of such technologies.

How did we get here?

- Agricultural revolution
- Print revolution
- Industrial revolution
- Digital revolution

What is the digital transformation process?

• Drivers	• Opportunities	• Challenges
❖ Market competition	❖ Enhanced customer experience	❖ Legacy systems
❖ Customer expectations	❖ Operational efficiency	❖ Cybersecurity risks
❖ Technology advancements	❖ Innovation	❖ Skills gap
❖ Business agility	❖ Data monetization	❖ Change management
❖ Cost efficiency	❖ Agility and scalability	❖ Data privacy concerns
❖ Data-driven insights	❖ Ecosystem collaboration	❖ Interoperability issues

Figure 2.1 Defining digitalization and the digital transformation process requires answering some fundamental questions

If that is not enough and the pace and volume of the digital sphere still feels daunting, remember that this is nothing new. The classic Greek thinkers also debated about the changeable nature of the world they knew and resorted to Sophia for an answer.

Heraclitus, a pre-Socratic philosopher, developed the idea of *panta rhei* or "everything flows," famously saying:

No man ever steps in the same river twice, for it's not the same river and he's not the same man.

Heraclitus is supposed to have written one single book, a papyrus roll he deposited in the great temple of Artemis at Ephesus, but only fragments of his work survived, often preserved by references made by other philosophers. Still, it's clear he was not a congenial person; he criticized some of the most famous classical authors like Homer and Hesiod, as well as the philosophers Pythagoras and Xenophanes, and had an entrenched disdain for the masses and his fellow men who, he thought, lacked the understanding to grasp his theories: .

Other men are unaware of what they do when they are awake just as they are forgetful of what they do when they are asleep.

Change Through Opposites + Stability Through Logos

Despite his controversial standing, Heraclitus did tap into a basic gauge of human anxiety when he looked at how the world is in a perpetual state of flux where change is the only constant. This change, he argued, arises from the tension between opposites. As day turns into night, hot becomes cold, and life eventually transitions to death, the world changes but also progresses. The interplay of opposites ultimately creates harmony in the world and prevents stagnation.

This dichotomy is more limited in the digital sphere but is also present. The tension between opposites comes from old and new, obsolete and relevant. Because the digital industry is a functional, purely utilitarian system where performance is rewarded, new technologies, services and systems that enhance the industry are adopted and old ones are discarded. Amazon Prime's 1-day delivery system is possible through the ruthless application of a process that increases the effectiveness of the purchase process, from online orders to fulfillment to delivery. Is this system "good" or "better" than what came before? It puts tremendous pressure on the different human components present on the chain, from warehouse workers to delivery service employees, but it does satisfy customers so "goodness" does not come into account. It is newer and more effective, so it replaces the previous system, thus bringing change, just as Heraclitus indicated.

But Heraclitus went beyond the theory of *panta rhei* or constant change. He proposed that change is not random and that there exists an underlying order or principle (*logos* meaning "word," "reason," or "principle" from where our word "logic" comes from) governing the universe. This rational principle ensures that change is not chaotic but follows a defined law. By aligning oneself with the *logos*, a person can gain a sense of order and meaning in a world of constant change.

In the digital space, interconnectivity, adaptability, and performance are key digital attributes but cannot quite be considered the central *logos*. Innovation does. Innovation—creating new ideas and solutions—is the driving principle and powers the digital world's constant evolution because it provides:

- Progress and growth.
- Efficiency and productivity.
- Problem-solving and interconnectedness.

Surviving Change in the Digital Age

Heraclitus' philosophy is, in short, one of observation and acceptance of the natural world. Because the digital transformation process is not a one-time event but rather an ongoing process, the learning from his theories is to view transformation as a dynamic journey rather than a fixed goal. And that is the mindset that encourages a culture of continuous innovation, which is the *logos* of the digital sphere.

Businesses and organizations are bound to encounter internal resistance to digital change. Fear of the unknown, attachment to familiar processes, those are natural reactions when facing a complex process of change but that does not mean they are justifiable responses. *Panta rhei* is there to help us reframe resistance as something natural but also as something that needs to be surpassed to grow and develop.

If there are three key learnings that we can extract from Heraclitus, they would be:

1. Improve continuously
   Heraclitus understood that nothing remains static, which can create tension, but consistent improvement mitigates its impact. People and organizations need to constantly update their skill sets via continuous learning to stay relevant in a world of rapid change. This is not just about learning new tools; it's about cultivating a mindset of continuous improvement, recognizing that change is the only constant.
2. Embrace adaptability
   Heraclitus saw change as an inherent part of existence. Rather than fearing disruption, we should recognize it as an opportunity. New technologies like AI, automation, and blockchain are not threats to be avoided; they are forces of change that can be harnessed for growth. Adaptability means being open to new possibilities, experimenting with new approaches, and finding innovative ways to create value in the face of disruption.
3. Build for sustainability
   Heraclitus' Sophia was about seeing the deeper pattern of change and not reacting to each small change. This translates to organizations needing to focus on long-term sustainability rather than short-term fixes. Instead of reacting impulsively to every new trend, there is a need to focus on building scalable solutions that can evolve alongside the business. This means investing in technologies that are not only effective today but also adaptable to future needs (Figure 2.2).

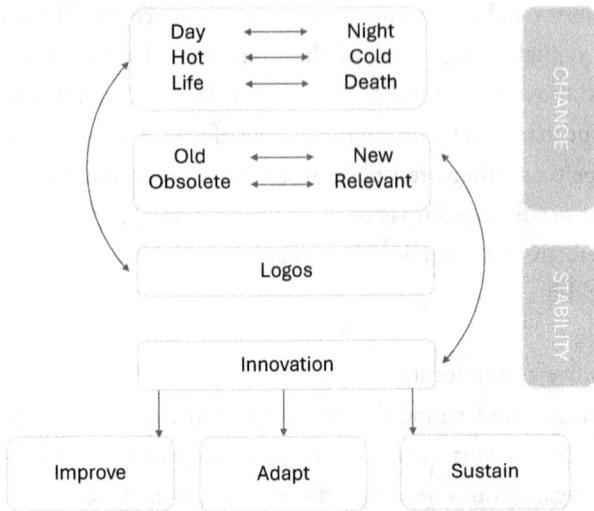

Figure 2.2 Heraclitus' model for stability and change can be applied to the digital sphere

CHAPTER 3

The Tools of Hephaestus: Big Data, IoT, AI, and Cloud Computing

Digital Is as Digital Does

Picture this: You are visiting a new country for work. First thing in the morning, you tap through e-mails on your phone. Want to see what is happening back home? You pull up your local news online. Stepping out of the hotel, you navigate the unfamiliar streets with a GPS app or get a ride with a familiar ride-sharing service. Between meetings, you are sharing how the trip is going, you message the family or post for your friends on social media. Too tired to go out for dinner? A food delivery app solves that. The amazing thing is, you're probably using the same catalogue of tools you use at home—Google Maps, Uber, WhatsApp—no new downloads, needed. It just works.

We call these services "digital." They're fast, need the Internet, live on our phones, and require logins. They look digital and feel digital. But what really makes them digital? We could say that they are of a format that is represented by discrete values, typically in a binary code of 1s and 0s, but that is a bit dry an explanation. What's that magic we all feel but struggle to define? What makes something "digital"?

When new consumer technologies started appearing in the mid-1990s and their connectivity ramped up with the widespread use of the Internet and the first data-guzzling mobile phones later in the decade, the label "digital" was a useful way of distinguishing them from the previous, existing technology of the time, like VHS tapes, vinyl records, terrestrial TV. Never mind that some of those old things used digital tech behind the scenes, for production and distribution. What mattered was the feeling and the term "digital" was a handy name to differentiate the efficient world of bursting Internet platforms, downloadable files, and sleek iPods from something that suddenly, seemed to us mechanical, clunkier, or maybe even slightly archaic: the old VCR under the TV, the Walkman you couldn't fit in your pocket, or the typewriter on the desk.

Digital products quickly replaced their analog predecessors, like the film camera bowing to the digital one, thanks to some key advantages:

- Better signal representation:
  Analog technology works on continuous signals like waves, which are prone to interference, while digital technology uses discrete signals (0s and 1s).
- Noise immunity:
  One of the big drawbacks of analog technologies like vinyl players, VCRs, and tape players was their tendency to mechanical noise and signal degradation compared to silent digital products with no mechanical moving parts.
- Versatility:
  While consumer analog technology was mainly applied to audio and video transmission, digital opened up a world of computing, data storage, and endless possibilities.
- Power Consumption:
  The mechanical working parts of analog technology meant higher power consumption than their digital equivalents.
- Cost:
  While initially pricier, digital products often had lower maintenance costs.

But technology doesn't stand still. So, what really makes something "digital" today? To understand that, we need to consider five core functionalities:

Digital Is Digitally Formatted

At its core, "digital" means data encoded in 0s and 1s. This binary format is incredibly flexible, enabling rapid and precise storage, retrieval, and transmission. As a result, digital information is far more adaptable than its analog counterpart. Consider a newspaper: Digitally, it can be updated instantly and reach a global audience. Your personal files, stored in the cloud, offer the same flexibility: accessible anywhere, editable, and shareable in real time.

Digital Is Connectable

Connectivity is the hallmark of digital. It is the reason your devices work together effortlessly, as anybody who has used an Apple watch, or a pair of Bluetooth headphones knows. And it's the foundation for future innovations in health care, energy, and beyond.

But connectivity is not just about devices, it also includes solutions that connect human resources like Slack, a digital messaging platform that links teams across the globe. Think about how a global project was run before the digital age; communication was done via mail or fax, and the fastest channel was the telephone which has no visual component. There was no way for two teams at different ends of the globe to collaborate in real time. Digital platforms have become indispensable for companies that work on synchronized projects and need to maintain connectivity across different time zones and departments.

Digital Is Data-Driven

Data is the lifeblood of digital technologies. It fuels decision making, streamlines processes, and personalizes experiences. When used effectively, data unlocks insights and creates seamless user journeys. Look at Amazon: They analyze your purchase history, browsing, and cart activity to recommend products you will like, boosting sales with every click. Netflix does the same, curating personalized recommendations based on your viewing habits, keeping you engaged. And it doesn't stop there. Data drives decisions on everything from website design to customer support, ensuring a smooth and tailored experience.

Digital Is Innovative

The digital space is a vast wheel of interconnected pieces. Developments in one area carry over to other companies because digital technologies are mutually reliant and constantly evolving; they leverage each other to drive innovation. Each new advancement builds on existing capabilities, unlocking new opportunities for businesses. Take Tesla, a pioneer in electric vehicles. Their cars aren't just powered by advanced batteries; they leverage AI and IoT sensors for semiautonomous driving. Tesla's progress hinges on advancements in all these areas, which in turn drives innovation for its partners and suppliers.

Digital Is Scalable

Digital's inherent flexibility translates to incredible scalability. Businesses can effortlessly adjust their capacity and operations, without massive investments. And because digital businesses can operate globally, scalability is built in. Companies like Amazon Web Services (AWS) leverage this, offering on-demand cloud infrastructure. Businesses can scale storage and computing power up or down as needed, making AWS a lifeline for startups and global giants alike. This means handling peak traffic without buying physical servers.

So, what makes something digital? What defines something as digital, not just in the technological sense but in a transformative one, is its ability to exist in a digitally formatted structure, be connected, utilize data, drive innovation, and achieve scalability.

Hephaestus and the Tools of Innovation

Some people don't have any luck, even gods.

Consider Hephaestus, the Greek god of blacksmiths, craftsmanship, and fire who, despite the talents that gained him the title, was not known for his beauty. Mythology portrays him as being the ugliest of the Pantheon, but what he lacked in good looks, he made up with his incredible skill in creating various mechanical and magical devices.

He is often depicted as handicapped, with myths suggesting either he was born with a pronounced limp, or it was the result of a mishap when his mother Hera, disgusted by his appearance, threw him from Mount Olympus. And on top of that, his wife Aphrodite had a very public affair with Ares, the god of war.

So being unsightly, disabled and scorned, Hephaestus focused on developing his creative genius. The very traits that set him apart became the fuel for his unparalleled craftsmanship. He would labor at his forge, day in and day out, the uneven gait forcing him to rely on ingenuity to develop intricate mechanisms, automated assistants, and tools that compensated for his physical limitations.

Hephaestus had to think differently, had to solve problems with precision and cleverness because he couldn't rely on the same physical prowess as the other gods. So he resorted to *metis*, the idea of cunning intelligence capable of adapting to intricate challenges.

A Patron Saint for Tech Wizards Everywhere

Two things make the figure of Hephaestus relevant (and quite inspiring) in the context of digital transformation.

On one side, the approach he took to problem-solving is very aligned with our modern one. *Metis* can be equated to "disruptive innovation." Rather than competing with the rest of the gods in their terms, his limitations lead him to develop entirely new technologies. And that is what the tools of digital transformation are about: Developing adaptive systems to navigate and solve complex problems.

More nuance is the significance of his figure as it relates to the social status of the "Technician." Despite his skill, Hephaestus often occupied a liminal space among the gods. He was respected for his craft and usefulness but often marginalized due to his physical appearance, which reflects the historical tension between those who create and those who use.

While engineers, data scientists and analysts have always been critical parts of industrial development, in many ways they tooled in the shadows, unseen and unheard. The democratization of technology, the larger dependency of companies on data and software and the increased visibility of stories about tech startups, AI breakthroughs, and data-driven innovations have captured the public's imagination, making these professions more visible and desirable.

Larry Page and Sergey Brin (from Google/Alphabet), Bill Gates (from Microsoft), and Jeff Bezos (from Amazon) are just a few of the entrepreneurs with almost rock star-like status who worked in the programming and technical infrastructure of their respective companies while still attaining incredible social popularity.

Today, a digitally savvy Hephaestus would probably surpass Ares in Aphrodite's eyes. In a world that prizes innovation and specialized knowledge, Hephaestus's tech wizardry would be far more appealing than the chaotic aggression of the god of war.

The Big Four

We will go back to Hephaestus but let us look now at the tools of the trade in digital transformation. While numerous digital technologies are vital, four stand out as foundational based on the characteristics of digitalization that we mentioned:

- The one that enables data-driven solutions: big data and analytics.
- The one that enables connectivity: Internet of Things (IoT).
- The one that enables innovation: artificial intelligence (AI).
- The one that enables data usage and scalability: cloud computing.

Big Data and Analytics

There were 5 exabytes of information created between the dawn of civilization through 2003, but that much information is now created every two days.

—*Eric Schmidt, Executive Chairman, Google*

We said it before; the digital world runs on data. It's the fuel and source of profits, a raw material that generates wealth if applied properly.

And data, digital data, has indeed gone big. If you read that quote from Mr. Schmidt, please consider the implications there. What he is saying is that all human knowledge that has been penciled down—every book, manuscript, map, image, and music partiture; every piece of paper, vellum, papyrus or parchment where mankind has scribbled since the invention of the written system up until the early 2000s—fits in the measure of 5 exabytes. The fact that all our social media posts and pictures, all text messages, videos, online comments, and e-mails from our smartphones regularly generate a similar amount is breathtaking. Whether that massive data trail translates to quality is another question entirely.

While the exact data volume before and after the early 2000s is debated, and the 5 exabyte figure may be approximate, it effectively conveys the sheer explosion of data in recent decades.

Big data refers to the large volumes of structured, unstructured, and semistructured data generated at high velocity by all the digital systems we use. From social media interactions to Internet of Things (IoT) devices, it can seem overwhelming, but like crude oil, it holds immense potential. When refined through analytics, big data transforms into actionable insights, empowering businesses to make smarter decisions, optimize operations, and gain a decisive competitive advantage.

As processing power surges, the label "big data" is becoming increasingly fluid. Datasets once deemed massive may now be considered routine. The word choice between "big data" and just "data" ultimately hinges on context, with the lines often blurring. The distinction comes down to the scale and complexity. We might just refer to everyday data tasks as "data," but when diving into the vast, complex datasets that power things like AI and machine learning, "big data" is a useful term to capture that scope and scale.

The 5 V's

Big data is often defined by five essential characteristics, also known as the "5 V's": volume, velocity, variety, veracity, and value. These dimensions point to both the opportunities and challenges that big data faces, but are worth considering because they come into play for any company looking to build a data-driven foundation for its business.

- Volume: Big data involves massive quantities of data from diverse sources. Just a company like Facebook generates over 4 petabytes of data daily, encompassing everything from user posts to multimedia interactions.
- Velocity: The speed at which data is generated and processed is crucial for real-time or near-real-time analytics. Take Visa: they handle over 65,000 transactions per second. Without the ability

to process this data at lightning speed, they couldn't instantly detect fraud and maintain secure transactions. Velocity is the key to immediate action.

- Variety: Not all data comes in the same format of neat rows and columns; it's a mix of structured, unstructured, and semistructured data. Netflix exemplifies this. They need to analyze user preferences (structured), video content (unstructured), and reviews (semistructured) to deliver those spot-on recommendations. Variety is key to personalization.

- Veracity: For most companies, their proprietary data sets are the ultimate source of truth so ensuring data accuracy, reliability, and quality is critical for meaningful insights. A data management policy that allows for proper handling is also key. Medical data, for example, because of its sensitivity, needs to be under stringent data governance and privacy protocols.

- Value: Ultimately, the goal of big data is to derive valuable insights that improve business outcomes. Retail giants like Walmart and Carrefour use analytics to optimize inventory, cut costs, and boost customer satisfaction by ensuring products are always in the right place at the right time.

Beyond its application, big data and analytics have become a lucrative business in themselves. Extracting those five key values requires a comprehensive suite of tools for storage, processing, and analysis. Where do businesses find these tools? Companies like Amazon Web Services and Google Analytics recognized this need early, developing scalable big data analytics solutions that now serve a vast segment of the digital industry.

A Very Useful Tool...

We've explored the technology and the value, but what does big data and analytics look like in practice? Its flexibility means applications are virtually limitless. Here are just a few:

- Business Intelligence: Big data enables companies to generate detailed reports and visualizations to track performance and inform decision making. Food and beverage companies, for example, use analytics to optimize supply chains and ensure product availability in key markets.

- Customer Analytics: Retailers use data to understand customer behavior and deliver personalized marketing. Target famously used big data to predict when customers were at different life stages (single, young family, retiree, etc.), sending them targeted offers based on different purchasing patterns.

- Fraud Detection: Financial institutions harness big data to detect suspicious patterns and prevent fraud. If you pay with your personal credit card while traveling to a foreign country, you may receive a notification alerting you. That is your card provider's analytics at play, detecting an unusual geolocation to flag suspicious transactions and reduce fraud risks across its global network.

- Health Care Analytics: Predictive analytics in health care is a huge area of development in the data and analytics field. Medical big data can identify patients at risk of serious conditions, enabling early intervention but also anticipate outcomes and enhance treatment. A more effective health care system not only benefits people but also reduces the resource strain and monetary burden of social welfare systems.

- Supply Chain Optimization: Predictive models help companies manage inventory and streamline logistics. A company like Amazon would be unable to forecast consumer demand, optimize warehouse locations, and enhance delivery efficiency without big data.

...Which Comes with Some Strings Attached

If Socrates had been able to look at what big data and analytics can do, he may have thought it was a supernatural device. A tool that can predict, quite accurately, what people will do? A tool that can create wealth out of thin air and direct the direction of large organizations?

Considering what we know of the Greek philosopher, it's very likely his next question would have been around the challenges and ethical considerations of such a capable tool. And he would not have been wrong, while big data and analytics present numerous opportunities, they also introduce a substantial set of challenges.

- Privacy and Consent: The collection and use of personal information without informed consent is a major concern. If users don't know how their data is being used, this can lead to privacy violations.
- Bias and Discrimination: The algorithms that generate all those valuable insights lack human sensitivity around social issues. A pure utilitarian use of analytics can perpetuate or even amplify biases present in the datasets they use.
- Transparency: If it is difficult for users to understand and control how their data is being collected, processed, and used, then the company or organization has transparency issues that it needs to address.
- Surveillance and Misuse: The potential for companies and governments to monitor and misuse data is a significant ethical concern that can lead to a loss of privacy.
- Data Quality and Governance: Ensuring data accuracy, consistency, and regulatory compliance is crucial.
- Security and Privacy: Closely related to the previous point, protecting sensitive data from breaches and ensuring compliance with government regulations is not only a legal requirement but an ethical one.

Besides the human and ethical impact, other technical considerations also have to be taken into account:

- Integration and Interoperability: The challenge of integrating data from disparate sources is a significant hurdle in data analysis. Seamless integration and interoperability are vital for global companies seeking to merge data from international operations, marketing, and supply chains to get a complete picture of their performance.
- Scalability and Performance: As data volumes expand, systems must scale efficiently without compromising performance. The

data and analytics process is never static but in continuous flux; thus, it requires continuous supervision.

The Internet of Things

The Internet of Things is transforming the everyday physical objects that surround us into an ecosystem of information that will enrich our lives.

From refrigerators to parking spaces to houses, the Internet of Things is bringing more and more things into the digital fold every day, which will likely make the Internet of Things a multi-trillion dollar industry in the near future.

—Price Waterhouse Cooper

Going back to Hephaestus, the handy Greek god of blacksmiths, one of his major accomplishments was the creation of the automatons, mechanical beings that could perform tasks independently. The most famous automaton was Talos, a giant bronze man designed to protect the island of Crete. Talos was said to patrol the island's shores and defend it from invaders by throwing massive boulders or heating his metal body and embracing enemies to burn them. Less spectacular, but probably more practical, were the *keladones* or golden handmaidens who assisted Hephaestus in his workshop. They were crafted to be incredibly lifelike and helped the blacksmith with his forging work. They were described as having intelligence, speech, and movement.

It may seem we are talking about robots here, but Hephaestus was looking to transform his workshop and forge into the equivalent of a car factory where a set of machines completed repetitive tasks in an assembly line. The two key skills Hephaestus installed in his automatons are autonomy and interconnection.

They could perform tasks independently but also work together, communicating with each other and making decisions on the spot. If an anvil dropped or another Greek god came in asking to have their chariot fixed, the workshop didn't come to a standstill; the *keladones* adapted and fixed the problem, saving Hephaestus time and worry.

The total was more than the sum of the parts, just like the Internet of Things (IoT).

The Internet of Things refers to a transformative network of interconnected physical devices that collect, transmit, and act upon data from their environments. We are surrounded by these devices, from smart thermostats in homes to fitness trackers and sophisticated industrial machinery. The IoT enables devices to communicate with each other and central systems in real time, allowing for unprecedented automation, efficiency, and data-driven decision making.

A Good Idea, Well Executed

The roots of IoT date back to the 1980s, when researchers experimented with connecting vending machines to the Internet to track stock levels. However, Kevin Ashton coined the term "Internet of Things" in 1999, envisioning a future where everyday objects would collect and share data. Over the past two decades, advancements in sensor technology, wireless communication, and cloud computing have accelerated IoT's growth.

The IoT is built on several core components that allow devices to interact and deliver value.

- Sensors and Actuators: At the heart of IoT are sensors and actuators. Sensors are the data gatherers, measuring everything from temperature and motion to humidity. Actuators are the action takers, responding to that data by, say, adjusting a valve or flipping a switch. Imagine a smart lighting system like Philips Hue. Sensors detect motion and ambient light, while actuators adjust the lights accordingly, optimizing energy use and saving you money.
- Connectivity: Connectivity is the lifeline of IoT. Devices use protocols like Wi-Fi, Bluetooth, and Zigbee to transmit data. Without reliable connections, these systems are useless. In a home setting, devices typically connect via Wi-Fi to a central platform, allowing for remote control through smartphones.
- Data Processing and Analytics: Data is the heart of any digital system, and IoT is no exception. Once collected, data must be

processed to extract meaningful insights. This processing can happen in the cloud or at the source. Companies like Siemens use IoT and advanced analytics in their factories to monitor machinery in real time, optimize production schedules, and slash energy consumption.

All Around You

All digital technologies work to transform back-end industries and front-end consumer applications, but IoT is the silent transformer, reshaping both industries and our daily lives. While other digital technologies work behind the scenes, IoT weaves itself into our routines, often unnoticed. Some of the most common applications of IoT include:

- Smart Homes: IoT-enabled devices automate your living space, from utilities to appliances. Imagine controlling your lights, locks, and even your washing machine with voice commands or a tap on your phone. It's all about convenience and seamless management.
- Wearables and Health Care: IoT is revolutionizing health care through remote monitoring and personalized care using wearable devices. Most connected wearables offer health features like heart rate monitoring, ECGs, and fall detection. In some cases they can alert emergency services if necessary.
- Smart Cities: IoT technology is transforming urban environments by improving traffic management, waste collection, and energy efficiency. Applied to real-time traffic monitoring and smart street lighting, IoT can improve urban living and reduce energy consumption.
- Industrial IoT (IIoT): In industries like manufacturing, agriculture, and logistics, IoT enables real-time monitoring of machinery and assets. This does not only apply to sophisticated hi-tech factories; agricultural machinery with IoT sensors can provide farmers with real-time soil moisture data to optimize water usage and increase crop yields through precision farming.

- Transportation and Logistics: IoT enables enhanced fleet management, vehicle tracking, and supply chain optimization. A logistics carrier like DHL employs IoT-enabled tracking systems to monitor the condition of sensitive shipments like pharmaceuticals, ensuring that goods arrive in optimal condition.

Risks and Benefits

The nature of IoT inherently raises significant concerns surrounding security and privacy. The interconnected and wireless systems that link various devices expose them to potential cyberattacks, and while unauthorized access to personal data is bad enough, please consider the implications when these connected devices control essential utilities and services like water supplies, energy distribution, or traffic signals. In 2016, a cyberattack of a malware program called Mirai exploited poorly secured IoT devices to form a massive botnet and caused widespread Internet outages.

If security is a challenge, interoperability is another one and looms large in the IoT sector. With numerous manufacturers and varying standards, achieving seamless communication between different IoT devices can prove difficult. Some initiatives like Matter, a smart home connectivity standard, have tried to tackle this issue by enabling cooperation among devices from different manufacturers, but it is still a work in progress.

And things are likely to become more complex in both areas as the adoption of IoT continues to surge. The complexity and scalability of managing millions of devices will grow exponentially while the vast amounts of data generated by these devices require more and more advanced systems for storage, processing, and analysis. Some companies are looking at this and, although all data is valuable, will have to set prioritization parameters to ensure that only the most pertinent information is processed in real time.

From a user perspective, we should also be thinking about some ethical and societal considerations. The sensors in our car and our fitness device may be very useful but they have become so integrated into everyday life that they can erode privacy. If your devices know where you are at any point, what you like to do and who you spend your time too, the risk of surveillance and the question of data ownership are just not theoretical. Imagine a smart city aiming to enhance urban infrastructure, it may be collecting data to understand traffic and transportation flows as well as population behavior patterns to improve quality of life but that same data in the hands of an authoritarian regime would have the opposite effect.

Looking to the future, it does seem everything around IoT will be more complex as several key trends are poised to shape its trajectory.

- 5G networks: This will be a critical development, promising faster and more dependable connectivity that is essential for the growing number of IoT devices. 5G-connected factories, where ultralow latency enables real-time production adjustments, significantly boosting efficiency.
- AI and machine learning: The integration of artificial intelligence and machine learning into IoT systems is driving smarter automation and informed decision making. If AI can learn user preferences over time, it will ultimately optimize things like energy use and home comfort.
- Blockchain technology: It is being investigated as a means to bolster security and transparency within the IoT space, particularly in supply chains. IBM's Food Trust blockchain platform illustrates this potential, using IoT and blockchain to trace food products from farm to table.

Whatever technological developments influence IoT moving forward, they will need to be backed by equally significant ethical and regulatory considerations. The European Union took the lead on this with its General Data Protection Regulation (GDPR) by setting a global precedent for data privacy and mandating that businesses handle IoT with the same transparency and compliance as any other sensitive dataset.

Hephaestus's automatons did not change the Greek classical world. They were a curiosity and an impossible fiction. But IoT is not. Connected devices have the potential to profoundly impact society and people in unprecedented ways. As the technology continues to evolve, its applications, challenges, and ethical considerations will play a critical role in our future.

Artificial Intelligence and Machine Learning

We will have, for the first time, something smarter than the smartest human. It's hard to say exactly what that moment is, but there will come a point where no job is needed.

—Elon Musk, Tesla and SpaceX entrepreneur

Hephaestus's *keladones* would come in handy when talking about artificial intelligence (AI). Thinking humanlike constructs that are there to help their creators? That seems like the very definition of AI as a system capable of performing tasks that require simulated intelligence (decision making, problem-solving, pattern recognition, etc.). But I don't think that is the case. What the god of fire was aiming to do was automate his environment in a connected, intelligent way; he was not looking for intelligence itself.

The best classic Greek parallel for AI is, I think, not Hephaestus's automatons but the Oracle of Delphi. In ancient Greece, oracles were revered as the voices of the gods, providing divine insights and prophecies. The Oracle of Delphi was a major power player that delivered instructions in cryptic pronouncements, guiding individuals and states. Oracles in general were seen as possessing a mystical connection to divine knowledge and the one in Delphi, particularly so, to the point that was often considered the center of the known world. The Oracle was only available for consultation on one day of each month and the consultation procedure involved a long waiting period, expensive sacrifices, and purification in the Castilian Spring. The oracular pronouncements that resulted were far from straightforward; they needed skilled priests to decode their meanings,

But the results must have been worth it. Even the historian Herodotus mentions the Oracle's words in his *Histories*:

I know the number of grains of sand and the extent of the sea; I understand the deaf-mute and hear the words of the dumb.

Modern AI systems analyze vast amounts of data to offer predictions and insights that seem almost magical. And just like the oracles of old, AI's insights can leave you scratching your head when it comes to interpreting their meaning, especially if the underlying algorithms are complex and their workings opaque.

From a secular standpoint, the Oracle of Delphi was an institution that leveraged religious beliefs and rituals to provide guidance and maintain social order. It didn't speak to the gods, it didn't have access to a supernatural body of knowledge; it worked with whatever data was available (political status quo, economic and social patterns, etc.) and offered alternative views and connections in that data that its petitioners might not have otherwise reached.

Just like AI does.

The Long Road to Intelligence

Artificial intelligence (AI) has long fascinated humanity, and within this vast field, machine learning (ML) stands out as a revolutionary subset. ML focuses on enabling machines to learn from data and improve their performance over time without being explicitly programmed. Together, AI and ML are not just transforming the digital world; they are reshaping the very fabric of how businesses and societies operate.

The journey of modern AI began in the 1950s, with Alan Turing's question, "Can machines think?" and the early development of neural networks. These foundational ideas laid the groundwork, but it wasn't until the twenty-first century that significant breakthroughs occurred. The rise of big data, advancements in computing power, and the availability of large datasets propelled AI into the mainstream. Nowadays, AI is embedded in technologies ranging from virtual assistants to self-driving cars, marking it as one of the most transformative forces of our era. It sits in your GPS map app, in your weather forecast update and on the shopping website you use.

To grasp the essence of AI and ML, it's crucial to understand their foundational concepts. AI is the broader field concerned with creating intelligent systems, while ML is a specific method within AI that focuses on learning from data in three ways:

1. Supervised Learning: Where models are trained on labeled data to make predictions.

2. Unsupervised Learning: Where models identify patterns in unlabeled data, often used for clustering and anomaly detection.
3. Reinforcement Learning: Where models learn through trial and error, receiving rewards or penalties for actions (commonly applied for gaming AI and robotics).

ML relies on three essential components: data, algorithms, and models. Data serves as the primordial element for training; algorithms process that data and the resulting models are capable of making predictions or decisions.

AI and ML applications span across industries; They may not be the thinking personalities we have seen in novels and films, but they solve complex problems, improve decision making, and drive innovation.

- Natural Language Processing (NLP): This allows systems to understand and generate human language. Most of the translation services online employs deep learning to enhance translation accuracy, while AI-driven chatbots, like ChatGPT, facilitate conversational customer service interactions.
- Computer Vision: AI interprets and analyses visual information, enabling machines to "see." Vehicle autopilot systems use computer vision to detect obstacles, navigate roads, and make real-time driving decisions, pushing us closer to fully autonomous vehicles. Later down the road, this capability would be key for achieving fully functional automatons and other constructs with autonomous movement capable of making real-time decisions based on sensor input and other data.
- Predictive Analytics: One of the most utilized AI capabilities. AI models use historical data to forecast future outcomes. Amazon leverages predictive analytics to optimize its supply chain, anticipating product demand and adjusting inventory for timely delivery.
- Health Care: AI is used in health care to facilitate faster, more accurate diagnoses and personalized treatment plans.
- Finance: AI is applied in algorithmic trading, fraud detection, and credit scoring. JPMorgan's COiN platform uses AI to analyze legal documents, thus reducing the scope for human error.

- Marketing and Advertising: AI can already generate visual and video creative content that is as relevant as anything made directly by a person. In parallel, AI algorithms can analyze user behavior to serve highly targeted ads, enhancing campaign relevance and conversion rates.

The Price We Pay the Oracle

While AI and ML offer immense benefits, they also present significant challenges, including data quality, ethical concerns, and system robustness.

Any AI model's results are only as good as what we pour into it, so they depend on high-quality, representative data. If there are faults at origin, if the data is biased or incomplete, predictions may be inaccurate or unfair. For instance, facial recognition systems have faced criticism for racial and gender biases, leading companies like IBM to review their development. Google, too, had to pause its Gemini AI tool after it produced results depicting historical figures—including popes, the founding fathers of the United States, and Vikings—in various improbable ethnicities and genders.

Many AI models, especially deep learning systems, act as "black boxes," making it difficult to interpret their decisions. Just as with the Oracle of Delphi, complex results need to be interpreted and the demand for systems that can explain the decisions of the AI models is growing. DARPA, the U.S. Department of Defense research division, seeks to develop AI systems that offer understandable explanations to enhance accountability.

And then there is the human factor. Ironically, one of the major societal implications of the use of AI is that it is producing both talent shortage and job displacement at the same time. On one hand, the rapid growth of AI and the very specialization of the field has created a dearth of skilled professionals. Despite heavy investments, even large players like Google and Microsoft struggle to find enough qualified engineers to meet demand. On the other hand, there is an ongoing threat for jobs to be replaced by AI. At Amazon's AI-powered warehouses, which employ robots for tasks previously handled by humans, there is a legitimate debate about the future of jobs in logistics and fulfillment.

The key to a balanced development of AI systems seems, again, related to the human perspective brought by Sophia. Human–AI collaboration, where AI augments human decision making and creativity by automating repetitive tasks and allowing users to focus on higher-level activities is the way to dispel most of the current issues.

Cloud Computing

I don't need a hard disk in my computer if I can get to the server faster…carrying around these non-connected computers is byzantine by comparison.

—Steve Jobs, Late CEO of Apple

Of all the technologies we've discussed, cloud computing is perhaps the most ubiquitous and the one that best enables the others to power the digital transformation process. By allowing businesses to access and use computing resources (such as storage, servers, databases, and networking) over the Internet on an on-demand basis, cloud computing is essential for big data, IoT, and AI.

It provides the space where big data are stored and where analytics are conducted. Cloud computing shares the crucial capability of connectivity with the IoT, channeling information collected by devices into a centralized repository. For AI, it offers the necessary infrastructure, enabling AI models to train on extensive datasets and run complex computations, which are vital for machine learning due to the significant processing power and storage required.

Cloud computing is to the digital revolution what the railroads were to the expansion of the American frontier. Just as the railroads connected distant regions, facilitating commerce, communication, and the movement of people, cloud computing connects disparate data sources and services, enabling seamless integration, collaboration, and the flow of information across the digital landscape.

The one key advantage that cloud computing offers, and one that has leveled significantly the playing field so every business can be a digital business, is that it eliminates the need for companies to invest in and maintain expensive physical hardware, allowing them to scale their IT infrastructure dynamically and pay for resources only when they are used. It has become, in many ways, the democratizing cornerstone of digital transformation, empowering organizations to innovate faster, reduce costs, and achieve greater operational flexibility regardless of size.

Nothing to Do with Clouds, Actually

Historically, the concept of cloud computing can be traced back to the 1960s. The predominant model for computing services was the "data center" where users submitted jobs to operators to run on mainframes, but alternative visions contemplated the idea of computation being delivered as a public utility, which was a fairly revolutionary concept in the nascent industry. However, it wasn't until the early 2000s that cloud computing began to gain traction with the advent of companies like Amazon Web Services (AWS) and Google.

Over time, cloud computing was systematized into three service models, each with its own merits:

- Infrastructure as a Service (IaaS) provides virtualized computing resources such as virtual machines, storage, and networking. Microsoft Azure offers IaaS solutions that enable businesses to host applications and data on its cloud infrastructure.
- Platform as a Service (PaaS) offers a platform for developers to build, run, and manage applications without the complexity of managing the underlying infrastructure. Google App Engine is an example, enabling developers to build and deploy applications on Google's infrastructure, automatically managing servers and scaling resources.
- Software as a Service (SaaS) delivers software applications over the Internet on a subscription basis, removing the need for local installations and maintenance. Salesforce, a leading cloud-based customer relationship management (CRM) platform, provides businesses with tools to manage customer interactions and sales processes entirely online.

Cloud computing offers numerous advantages that have redefined business operations. Because of its pay-per-use model, businesses can reduce capital expenditures on hardware and infrastructure that is not only cheaper to set up and run, but can be scaled up or down based on demand to manage fluctuating workloads. If your company provides a service that sees spikes of use, you want to secure support at those periods but have a running cost that is more adjusted to your average consumption.

A key feature of cloud computing is accessibility and mobility. If you were a user of Microsoft Office programs like PowerPoint or Excel before 2011, you needed to be at your computer to work on that presentation. But after Microsoft released Office 365 as a cloud-based service, that physical dependency was removed. You can access the program from any computer with an Internet connection. Or think about Slack, a cloud-based communication platform now used widely as an instant messaging corporate tool which makes remote work more efficient and seamless. Before this solution, e-mail or telephone-based conferences were the fastest options for group work.

A final capability of cloud computing and something that makes it more appealing to companies than in-premise data support is disaster recovery and business continuity. Cloud providers offer backup and re-dundancy services that help businesses recover quickly from disruptions. In case of fire or an earthquake, you can be sure your systems will re-main operational during outages or emergencies, maintaining business capabilities.

Dark Clouds with a Silver Lining

While cloud computing presents tremendous benefits, it also poses challenges that businesses must navigate to ensure smooth adoption and operation.

- Security and Compliance: Protecting sensitive data in the cloud and ensuring compliance with regulations is critical. In 2019, Capital One experienced a significant data breach due to a mis-configured cloud service, exposing sensitive customer data and highlighting the importance of robust cloud security practices.
- Data Transfer and Bandwidth Costs: The cost of data transfer costs and network bandwidth can climb rapidly for companies handling large datasets.

- Vendor Lock-In: Relying heavily on a single cloud provider can make it difficult for businesses to switch providers or adopt a multicloud strategy if needed. Some companies like Dropbox, which services storage needs for private users, decided to go all in and transition from AWS services to its own infrastructure but that is an expensive route to follow.
- Performance and Reliability: It is critical to ensure consistent performance and minimize downtime in cloud environments. In 2020, Slack faced outages due to issues with its cloud provider, highlighting the need for reliable infrastructure to maintain business operations.
- Integration Complexity: Integrating cloud services with existing on-premises systems and ensuring compatibility across platforms can be complex. Auto companies are particularly susceptible given the scale of their operation and service history. Volkswagen has worked to integrate AWS cloud infrastructure with its legacy systems, aiming to create a unified manufacturing platform.

Despite any potential challenges, the future of cloud computing remains exceptionally promising, as the industry evolves further driven by key trends: businesses are embracing hybrid cloud solutions to avoid vendor lock-in, edge computing is enabling real-time data processing, serverless computing is simplifying development, and cloud platforms are democratizing AI and machine learning.

And One Last Tool: Digital Twins

There is one addition to the tools available for digital transformation that is worth noting in this section: the digital twin.

Digital twins are virtual representations of a physical object or system. These are more than just a design tool or a simple 3D model; they are dynamic, virtual copies that mirror their physical counterparts in near real time. This is made possible by the convergence of the technologies discussed earlier in this chapter. IoT devices provide the sensory data, big data infrastructure handles the massive flow of information, AI algorithms process and analyze the data to generate insights, and cloud computing provides the scalability and accessibility needed to manage the entire process.

Imagine you are an engineer working with a Formula 1 team. Each car create for racing is unique and extremely expensive because they are hand-crafted to specific parameters to achieve peak performance. If things don't go as planned, the setback can cost the team a race or a championship.

So companies create sophisticated virtual models of the race car and its various systems using a combination of data from Computer-Aided Design (CAD) models, wind tunnel testing, and on-track sensor data. During races and test sessions, sensors on the car collect real-time data on parameters such as speed, acceleration, tire pressure, temperature, and aerodynamic performance. This data is then fed into the digital twin.

The primary purpose of digital twins in F1 is to optimize car performance. By simulating different scenarios and making changes to the virtual car, engineers can test and fine-tune setups, components, and strategies without the need for physical track time or risks to the physical model.

Beyond racing, the applications of digital twins are vast and varied, and they're transforming industries across the board:

- Manufacturing: Digital twins optimize production processes and predict equipment failures. Companies like General Electric (GE) use digital twins to monitor the performance of their jet engines and learn when maintenance is needed therefore reducing downtime.
- Health Care: In health care, digital twins are being used to create personalized treatment plans and simulate surgical procedures. Digital twins of organs or even patients can help doctors simulate the outcomes of different treatments, improving patient care and reducing risks.
- Smart Cities: Smart cities leverage digital twins to manage complex urban systems. They can be used to optimize traffic flow, energy consumption, and infrastructure maintenance. Singapore has developed a virtual model of the entire city to test new technologies and policies before implementing them in the real world.

As you can see, the key advantages of using digital twins are around performance metrics:

- Optimization: By simulating different scenarios, businesses can optimize operations, reduce waste, and improve efficiency.
- Prediction: Digital twins can predict potential problems or failures, allowing for proactive maintenance and preventing costly downtime.
- Innovation: They provide a safe environment for testing new ideas and designs, accelerating innovation and reducing risk.

However, the implementation of digital twins is not without its challenges. It requires significant investment in technology and expertise. Data security and privacy are also critical concerns, as digital twins collect and process vast amounts of sensitive information.

Despite these challenges, digital twins represent a powerful evolution in how we interact with and understand the physical world. Like the tools of Hephaestus, they extend our capabilities, allowing us to see beyond the surface and manipulate reality in the digital space.

Meaningful Tools

Ancient Greeks used mythology to imagine solutions to their world. Hephaestus with his creations and the Oracle with its cryptic pronouncements, were attempts to find wisdom from the divine,

We are not that different. We still reach out for wisdom and although our modern mythology is made of algorithms and data streams, and is more real and more influential, it can often be as inscrutable. The difference is that we are fully responsible for our creations and the true measure of our progress lies not just in the tools we craft, but in how we apply their use.

In using big data, IoT, cloud computing, and AI, we've seen how these technologies transform our daily lives. Ultimately, their impact will be determined by our collective wisdom and our application of Sophia.

CHAPTER 4

Epicurus the Sage and the Digital Experience

Digital Ataraxia and the Lessons of Epicurus the Sage

One of the strangest comic books out there must be the two-issue series *Epicurus the Sage*, written by William Messner-Loebs with art by Sam Kieth. Published by Piranha Press (an imprint of DC Comics) in 1989 and 1991, it came at a point of high experimentation in the medium and it's a satirical take on ancient Greek philosophy. The comic humorously portrays the philosopher Epicurus as the protagonist, traveling through ancient Greece alongside other famous figures like Plato, Aristotle, and even Alexander the Great. It was a very peculiar story told in a very peculiar format.

The comic blends philosophy, mythology, and slapstick humor but also offers a lighthearted critique of some of the ideas from the classical Greek era, and it is at its best when poking fun at the contradictions and personal neuroses of the different philosophers: Socrates is a bully, Plato is an insecure scholar, and Aristotle, a demagog. While Epicurus stands out as the voice of reason and moderation, a running joke in the series is how different characters make fun of his unorthodox philosophical principles, with Socrates saying at one point:

So, you really think that man becomes more noble through gluttony, fornication and getting drunk?

That is, of course, an oversimplistic take on the Epicurean concept of *ataraxia* or the pursuit of tranquility. *Ataraxia*, in Epicurean philosophy, is a state of freedom from anxiety and mental peace. Epicurus believed that the highest form of happiness was not found in fleeting pleasures or material wealth but in achieving a life free from pain (both physical and mental) and fear. For him, *ataraxia* was the ultimate goal of life, a serene state where one is undisturbed by worries, whether they stem from external circumstances or internal desires.

Epicurus taught that people often pursue unnecessary or excessive pleasures, thinking these will bring happiness. However, true pleasure is found in moderation and satisfaction of simple desires. The key to *ataraxia* is not overindulgence, but the ability to live without craving what we do not need. He also emphasized the importance of understanding and controlling our desires to maintain this state of tranquility.

Epicurus championed moderation and classified desires and pleasures into three types:

- Natural and necessary desires: These encompass fundamental needs such as food, shelter, and companionship. Meeting these desires brings contentment.
- Natural but unnecessary desires: These involve luxuries like fine food and comfort. Although they provide enjoyment, they are not crucial for happiness.
- Vain and empty desires: These pertain to the pursuit of wealth, power, or fame. Such desires are insatiable and often lead to anxiety.

By concentrating on fulfilling only the natural and necessary desires, one can achieve *ataraxia* while avoiding the disturbances caused by the latter categories.

Now, it may seem contradictory to apply such a balanced principle to the digital space, where moderation is often scarce, whether in online shopping, discourse, or the ostentatious display of wealth. However, when it comes to the experiences that consumers and users seek in the digital realm, *ataraxia*, tranquility, and freedom from anxiety are precisely what we all crave.

Online shopping is effective only when consumers are confident that products will be delivered as promised and their credit card information is processed securely. Instant messaging succeeds when users trust that their messages will remain private and not be intercepted. Similarly, cloud storage is reliable only when we are certain that our pictures and videos cannot be accessed by others without permission.

Without these assurances, digital experiences falter. Trust and peace of mind are not optional; they are the essential foundation upon which the digital space operates.

Epicurean Customer Support

The overall experience a user has when interacting with a digital product (a website, an app, or any type of software) is referred to as the digital user experience (UX). It is critical because, in a world of seemingly endless choices, attracting and retaining the attention of users determines the success or failure of a company.

This is easier said than done and many factors affect the user experience which is, after all, a dialogue of messages and signals between the consumer and the organization. It involves navigating a complex interplay of factors: Design, usability, reliability, convenience, performance, and content quality all contribute to the user's perception. A company that understands the background, interests, and profile of its audience is better positioned to craft a meaningful experience.

Therefore, tailoring digital experiences to specific audiences is crucial; an app for Brazilian users will diverge significantly from one intended for Vietnam, and a financial website will differ greatly from a travel platform. However, fundamental principles, echoing Epicurean ideals, remain universally applicable for businesses seeking to enhance user experience:

- Eliminate friction.
- Personalize it.
- Make it reliable.
- Add customer support.
- Provide value.
- Make it simple.

Eliminating Friction: Smooth, Intuitive Design

A key principle of *ataraxia* is removing sources of disturbance. On digital platforms, this is akin to eliminating friction points in user interfaces.

Customers feel at ease when platforms are intuitive, easy to navigate, and responsive.

Frustration over slow load times, complex navigation, or confusing layouts disrupts the flow. Therefore, a seamless, frictionless experience from browsing to checkout creates a digital environment that fosters tranquility and satisfaction.

Personalization: Tailoring Experiences to Minimize Decision Fatigue

Because of the versatility of digital technology, we, as consumers, are often spoiled for choices, but "more" does not always mean "better." It is important to personalize content and recommendations in a way that aligns with customer preferences but without overwhelming them with options that lead to decision fatigue.

Personalization added to simplicity links with the Epicurean principle of satisfying basic needs without overindulgence. Personalized content, product recommendations, and targeted offers that anticipate customer needs will reduce decision fatigue and create a sense of mental tranquility. Customers appreciate when platforms "know" what they want, leading to a smoother journey.

Consistency and Reliability: Stable and Predictable Services

Epicurean *ataraxia* emphasizes security; ensuring that one's fundamental needs are met dependably and consistently. Similarly, when a platform operates smoothly, free from crashes, glitches, or outages, it delivers a stable and predictable experience. This reliable performance in mobile apps, e-commerce platforms, and digital services nurtures a sense of security.

Empathetic Customer Support: Resolving Issues Without Stress

Epicurus believed that avoiding unnecessary pain was crucial to the human experience. In the digital world, this comes through customer support that resolves problems quickly, without adding stress.

When customers encounter issues with digital platforms, whether in billing, a broken link, or a technical glitch, the quality of the support they receive can either disrupt or restore their trust. An effortless, friendly customer service experience, particularly one that is empathic and human to human, restores balance and reduces any disturbance.

Ongoing Value and Reward: Sustained Satisfaction

Epicurus's idea of pleasure wasn't just about short-term gratification but sustained contentment. Digital solutions are only as good as the value they provide and such value is showcased on their long-term customer engagement strategies including loyalty programs, subscription benefits, and personalized ongoing communication.

It is crucial that the value proposition offered develops over time and matches the march of digital technology trends to stay relevant. If your company has long-format videos and consumers start gravitating toward short-format clips, you would need to find a way to address that to avoid attrition. When customers feel like they are receiving consistent value from a service or platform over time, they will stay engaged.

Balancing Simplicity with Fulfillment: Avoiding Overload

Epicurean philosophy teaches that true happiness lies in simple pleasures, and avoiding overconsumption. Similarly, digital platforms should aim for a balance between simplicity and fulfillment where less is more.

Overloading customers with too many options, overexposing them to ads, or adding complex features can lead to a sense of overwhelm. Instead, offering a clean, minimalist design with features that fulfill customer needs without excess creates an experience of digital ataraxia where simplicity leads to satisfaction.

To summarize, applying the Epicurean principles to the experience of your digital services could be as simple as following these three rules:

- Provide interactions that leave the user content rather than stressed.

- Provide technical standards that guarantee good design, data security, and system reliance.
- Provide personalized, thoughtful support that minimizes frustration.

The Broken Path of the User Journey: From Linear to Nonlinear

We mentioned that the digital user experience refers to the overall experience a user has when interacting with a digital product. Another key concept is the user journey which refers to the path a user takes to achieve a specific goal on a digital platform or environment.

When planning a trip on a site like Booking.com, your user experience is shaped by factors like site layout, hotel inventory, and booking ease. However, your navigation patterns are equally crucial for Booking.com. To optimize sales, they track not just completed bookings, but also your different interactions: how many properties you viewed, if you adjusted dates for better deals, and if you abandoned the booking process before payment.

All those points of engagement between the company and the user tell a story. An aggregated number of stories from different users gives companies insights into strengths and weaknesses, informing necessary improvements for continued success. So, the user journey sits at the heart of a compelling digital experience, and maximizing the effectiveness of the path from initial awareness to purchase will reduce attrition and loss of opportunity, as well as improve user satisfaction.

Before the digital age, the user journey was a simpler matter. It was not easy, mind you; companies and organizations still competed fiercely with each other to find, engage, and retain customers but the limited number of communication channels made it much more streamlined. Consumers visited a store, looked at the product, maybe went back home and slept on it, and eventually returned to the shop for purchase. Often, mass media played a significant role in influencing consumer decisions when a person saw an ad in a newspaper, heard it on the radio, or watched it on TV.

That linear model, with customers following a predictable path from awareness to purchase, has evolved into a nonlinear, omnichannel

experience. Today's consumers move seamlessly between online and offline touchpoints, engage with multiple channels, and expect consistency
across all of them. Think about the last purchase you made, maybe you
saw a product on Instagram, that was mentioned by a friend or promoted
by an influencer. Then you searched on Google, read reviews on Amazon, asked friends about it while having coffee, and finally purchased it
through the brand's website or at a brick-and-mortar store.

Find the Right Moment...

Here is a good rule of thumb for businesses that want to have a consistent conversation with users and know what message should be delivered
at each touch point: Understand the user's current stage within their
journey.

Look at some of the ads you receive online every day; many of them
are irrelevant but there may be a brand or two that tells you exactly what
you want to hear. It is very different to speak to somebody who has never
heard about your fancy new line of running shoes than to somebody who
is a registered member of your loyalty program and a regular buyer. The
former requires awareness-building while the latter allows for personalized messaging

Effective companies tailor their messages to these four stages of engagement for better results:

1. Awareness
   At this stage, customers become aware of a need or problem. This
   can happen naturally (I need a new pair of shoes) or through marketing efforts such as advertisements, social media posts, or word of
   mouth. If I see an Instagram ad for a fitness tracker, that may trig-
   ger my interest in monitoring my health.
2. Consideration
   In this stage, customers research and evaluate different products
   or services that can fulfill their needs. They compare options, read
   reviews, and seek recommendations. After discovering the fitness
   tracker, I may go to different websites, read user reviews, and watch
   YouTube videos to determine which model suits me best.

3. Decision

   The customer decides to purchase the product or service based on factors such as pricing, reviews, and user experience. I might be influenced by a limited-time discount or a positive review from a trusted source, which leads me to purchase the fitness tracker from an online retailer.

4. Post-Purchase

   Even after the purchase, the user's journey is not over. Post-purchase engagement is crucial for customer satisfaction and loyalty. Now that I have my fitness tracker, I may appreciate follow-up e-mails from the manufacturer with tips on how to use the product or offering other accessories.

A company's messaging can either guide a user through the purchase journey or derail it entirely. A premature discount offer during the awareness stage, when a user is unfamiliar with the product, is ineffective. Conversely, a generic ad during the final purchase consideration stage, when all research has been done, will likely fall short. So, it is up to the company to ensure that these moments of communication provide consistent, relevant, and engaging experiences to keep customers moving toward the final purchase.

Find the Right Place...

Where do you do all this? Within the digital sphere, various platforms serve as touchpoints for user engagement:

1. Websites

   A company's website is often the first point of contact for potential customers and therefore the storefront that displays all it has to offer. Website build and design have become more and more sophisticated over the years; a well-designed website goes beyond aesthetics as marketers analyze users' browsing behavior to understand what works and what doesn't.

   This involves responsive design, ensuring optimal viewing across all devices; search engine optimization (SEO) to ensure higher search rankings; intuitive user experience to enable easy navigation; engaging content to provide valuable information and attract users; and analytics, utilizing tools like Google Analytics to track performance.

2. Social Media

Since its appearance in the late 2000s (with Facebook and Twitter launched in 2006, and YouTube launched in 2007 as key players) social media has become an essential tool for user engagement. It drives brand awareness by expanding reach through organic posts and paid ads. The interactive nature of comments, messages, and content sharing—blog posts, videos, and images—fosters a more organic and natural connection compared to traditional websites.

3. E-mail Marketing

E-mail, the grandfather of digital communication, may feel obsolete in the private space but it remains a potent tool for direct communication. Successful e-mail marketing campaigns focus on segmentation, which divides the e-mail list into segments based on demographics, behavior, or preferences. Companies have many levers they can use to adjust e-mails to engage just in the right way: Personalization customizes e-mails to address the recipient by name and include relevant content while analytics can track who opened each mail, who clicked on the content included and who ended up purchasing the product.

4. Mobile Apps

If websites are the storefront of a company, apps are the personal shopper that makes your experience an excellent one. They build on each specific user's information and preferences to offer a seamless journey. Effective apps feature intuitive, user-friendly interfaces, deliver timely and relevant notifications, facilitate in-app purchases, offer loyalty programs to reward repeat customers, and provide offline functionality for seamless use even without Internet access.

5. Customer Support

Modern customer support may not be as exciting as flashy websites and hi-tech apps but it is the one space designed to provide efficient user assistance. It utilizes chatbots for instant responses and guided support, helpdesk software for organized ticket management and

issue resolution, self-service portals with FAQs and tutorials for independent problem-solving, and multichannel support across e-mail,
phone, live chat, and social media for comprehensive assistance.

Make It Count…

So, you are talking to the user at the right moment and finding them in
the right place. But competition out there is fierce. The scarcest currency
in the digital space is attention, user attention. All of us are bombarded
with information when we go online with hundreds of companies eager
to tell us a story or sell us a product. How can a company make sure that
its touchpoints are engaging enough so the user stays on board for the
duration of the journey? Some of these principles may be useful.

1. Make It Personal
   Personalization involves creating content, offers, and recommendations specifically tailored to a customer's preferences, behaviors,
   and demographics. By making the content relevant, much like how
   Netflix suggests movies and TV shows based on a user's viewing
   history, companies can significantly increase the likelihood of user
   engagement.
2. Make It Consistent
   An omnichannel strategy ensures that customers have a seamless experience across all touchpoints, whether they interact with a brand
   online or offline. Consistency is key to building trust and maintaining engagement throughout the customer journey.
       The cosmetic retailer Sephora has integrated its online store,
   mobile app, and physical stores in a way that customers can shop
   online, check product availability in-store, and redeem loyalty
   points across all channels.
3. Make It Logical
   Users share with you information that can and should be processed
   to improve the engagement and the overall experience. Leveraging
   customer data is critical for optimizing the customer journey. The
   conversation between an organization and a user should be heartfelt
   (meaning honest) but also logical and data-driven.

4. Make It Easy

UX design focuses on creating intuitive, easy-to-navigate interfaces that enhance user satisfaction. Are your functionality buttons hard to find? Are you laying out an easy path for the user's gaze to travel through the screen? A well-designed UX can make the difference between a customer completing a purchase or abandoning their cart.

And Automatize It

Both the consumer experience and the user journey present tremendous advantages but they necessitate tracking individual interactions across diverse channels, resulting in vast amounts of varied digital data.

We will be looking at how all that data can be organized and managed but first, let's review what types of tools you would need to have in your technology arsenal to optimize and manage user engagement.

1. Customer Relationship Management Systems:
CRM systems are platforms designed to manage customer interactions, track leads, and analyze data. They help companies understand the entire customer lifecycle, allowing for better engagement and retention strategies. A platform like Salesforce, which integrates sales, marketing, and customer support into one system, is a one-stop solution to get meaningful insights.

2. Marketing Automation Tools:
Marketing automation tools streamline the process of managing marketing campaigns. These tools help businesses automate tasks such as e-mail campaigns, and social media postings, and lead nurturing workflows, allowing teams to focus on strategy and creativity. HubSpot is one of those solutions and allows businesses to schedule and send personalized e-mails, run automated social media campaigns, and track customer behavior.

3. Customer Data Platforms:
A customer data platform (CDP) is a centralized database that collects and unifies customer data from multiple sources. It provides a complete view of the customer, allowing businesses to deliver personalized marketing and customer service experiences. It gathers

its data from various platforms, such as websites, mobile apps, and third-party integrations, and creates a unified customer profile.

4. Artificial Intelligence and Machine Learning:
   Artificial intelligence (AI) and machine learning (ML) are critical technologies for delivering personalized customer experiences. These technologies power chatbots, recommendation engines, and predictive analytics, enabling businesses to anticipate customer needs and offer relevant products or services in real time.

5. Analytics and Business Intelligence Tools:
   Analytics and business intelligence (BI) tools are essential for understanding customer behavior, measuring campaign performance, and calculating return on investment (ROI). These tools provide insights that help businesses optimize their digital experiences. Google Analytics is one of the most widely used tools out there for tracking website traffic and conversion rates.

The Path to Ataraxia Is Paved by Data

Picture this: It's a rainy Friday evening and you are going on your first date with someone you've met recently. You both arrive, umbrellas in hand, and although the conversation is a bit awkward at the beginning, you navigate through a maze of topics and, bit by bit, map out each other's interests and hobbies and the small café feels like a world apart.

As the evening progresses, you search for more common ground, bringing up new topics whenever the conversation threatens to lapse. There's a bit of uncertainty here but things are looking good and the night ends on a promising note, so you plan a second date. This time, it's an afternoon hike. The conversation flows effortlessly now; you share stories and discover similar passions. By the third date, you hit your stride and find comfort in each other's presence as the dialogue deepens.

Two things are happening here: With each date, you simultaneously deepen your understanding of one another and accumulate shared experiences, fostering a richer, more personal connection.

Now, imagine a twist in this tale. You arrive at the second date, only to find your partner looking at you with unfamiliar eyes. They recall nothing about you. You feel frustrated but dutifully you retrace the steps of your first conversation, talking about your likes and dislikes once more. Time slips away, and you regain the nice, warm feeling you felt on the first date. Then you meet for a third time and yet again, the other person remembers nothing. It's like living in a surreal dream, where the past doesn't exist, and the future never quite materializes. What do you do? Leave? Go through a new reset that prevents progress?

The first scenario reflects Epicurus's *ataraxia*; a serene state that comes from the simple pleasure of spending time with another person, getting to know them better. The second one, well, that is a frustrating endless loop out of the movie *Groundhog Day.* Such is the importance of memory and shared experiences in a relationship. Without them, every date becomes just another first date, with no richness or progress.

Now think if every single time you visit an app or website, you have to customize it to your taste. You have to include what time zone you are in, what region of the world, and what language you prefer. Or picture accessing your YouTube, Netflix, or Amazon account and seeing nothing there that matches your taste or sparks your interest and having to spend your time tailoring the channel. Even worse, imagine doing all that all over again the following day.

Without consumer data there to inform it, your favorite digital solutions would be like a nightmarish, ever-repeating first date.

In the digital space, your experience is improved because the system remembers what you like and dislike, where you are located, what time it is for you; it can infer what recommendations you will enjoy and which ones you will definitely not. Data makes that possible; user personal data, to be more specific.

Use data refers to any information that can be used to identify, contact, or locate an individual, and that companies collect, store, and analyze to enhance services and target recommendations. If it sounds just a bit too good to be true, it's because not all is rosy. The promise of personalized digital experiences, fueled by user data, often comes with a hidden cost: a Faustian bargain where convenience and tailored services are exchanged for potential manipulation, privacy erosion, and ethical data misuse.

We mentioned before that data is the fuel of the digital space. It is also the lifeblood of the digital experience; without it, creating truly meaningful online interactions is impossible. Even the most innovative companies, lacking this crucial information, can only produce generic, ineffective solutions.

The Many Shapes of Data

Not all data is created equal. Certain types of data provide a "stronger signal," meaning, they give a better understanding of who the user is and what they may be interested in.

The most relevant types of data about a user, ranked from generic to specific value, are as follows.

1. Demographic Data:
   Demographic data is basic user information such as age, gender, income, education, location, and occupation. It helps businesses understand the characteristics of their customer base and create messages that resonate with specific groups. For example, Nike might target teens through social media and professionals traditional media, emphasizing different product aspects.

   While very valuable, the digital space's reliance on demographics reflects television's legacy, where audience segmentation was primarily based on program viewership and corresponding demographic profiles. Television's broad format necessitated this approach, which has, to some extent, carried over into digital marketing.

2. Contextual Data:
   Contextual data considers the environmental and situational factors that influence consumer behavior. This includes information such as location, time of day, and even the device a consumer is using. You can see contextual data in action in any mapping application. Companies like Google use real-time location data to tailor information for the user but also to serve advertising for nearby restaurants or stores.

3. Behavioral Data:
   Behavioral data, particularly online browsing habits, offers significant insights into user interests and profiles. It tracks online actions, such as browsing history, purchase history, and content engagement. This data is vital for understanding real-time user interests.

Amazon leverages behavioral data to generate personalized product recommendations based on past searches and purchases, fostering a tailored shopping experience that promotes customer loyalty and repeat business.

4. Psychographic Data:

   Psychographic data, or lifestyle data, explores consumers' psychological traits, including values, attitudes, and interests. This data facilitates emotional connections by aligning company messaging with core values. For example, a car company uses lifestyle data to appeal beyond mere functionality, and a fashion brand sells not just clothing, but a desired identity. Outdoor apparel brands like Patagonia or The North Face attract environmentally conscious consumers by emphasizing sustainability and ethical practices.

5. Transactional Data:

   This type of data includes records of purchases, financial transactions, and interactions with a business. It is essential for understanding buying patterns, tracking sales trends, and predicting future revenue. A company that can look at transactional data to identify which products are frequently bought together and then use this information to create bundle offers or promotions that maximize sales would have a tremendous advantage.

Put Your Data to Work

Once consumer data is collected, it becomes a powerful tool for crafting more effective strategies and making informed business decisions. But in many aspects, this data is a raw and pliable construction material, like steel, concrete, sand, or bricks. How it is used depends on each company and their vision. Some may try to apply it to improve their services, others may focus on monetizing it to generate revenue.

Regardless of the case, the most common ways in which consumer data is crafted and used include the following.

1. Personalization:

   As we mentioned before, making it personal is the most relevant application of data. By tailoring messages, product recommendations, and content based on individual preferences and behavior, businesses can create more engaging experiences for their customers.

2. Targeted Advertising:

Targeted advertising allows businesses to reach specific audience segments with ads that resonate with their particular interests and needs. By using demographic, behavioral, and psychographic data, companies can ensure their ads are delivered to the right people at the right time. Both Google and Meta have created an ecosystem that leverages data to craft targeted advertising for the brands that purchase their services.

3. Predictive Analytics:

Predictive analytics uses historical data and machine learning algorithms to forecast future behavior, trends, and outcomes. This is invaluable for businesses anticipating customer needs and acting proactively. A clothing retailer might use predictive analytics to stock up on certain items that are likely to be in demand based on previous buying trends during certain seasons.

4. Customer Segmentation:

Customer segmentation involves grouping consumers into segments based on common characteristics, behaviors, or preferences. This enables businesses to create targeted strategies for each segment. A luxury hotel chain might segment its customers into categories like business travelers, honeymooners, and families, offering tailored packages and services to each group based on their unique needs and desires.

5. Attribution:

Attribution helps businesses understand how their engagement efforts are working (which channel or message is having the most impact). By tracking the customer journey and understanding the impact of each touchpoint, businesses can allocate resources to the most effective channels, remove the ones that don't perform and understand the cost-return of their strategies at every step.

The Magic Pyramid: Aristotle's Categories and Data Taxonomies

Figuring out data is a difficult thing to do.

Throughout history, people have sought to organize and categorize the world around them in order to gain a deeper understanding of how it functions. In Western intellectual history, the work of Aristotle has had an immense and lasting impact on how we approach classification.

Aristotle is widely recognized as one of the earliest philosophers to develop a structured system for classifying the observable world. He focused particularly on what he termed "entities," or "substances" (known as *ousia* in Greek), which he considered the fundamental existing things in the universe. This included a detailed attempt to categorize living organisms, which Aristotle grouped based on their inherent characteristics and observed behaviors. His efforts laid the foundation upon which subsequent biological classification systems would be built.

Aristotle proposed that understanding an entity requires examining its four causes.

1. Material Cause:
   This refers to the substance that something is made of. For example, the material cause of a statue is the marble or bronze from which it is sculpted.
2. Formal Cause:
   This is the design, form, or blueprint that something follows.
   For the statue, the formal cause is the shape or structure that the sculptor intends to create.
3. Efficient Cause:
   This is the agent or process that brings something into being. In the case of the statue, the efficient cause is the sculptor who carved the marble or bronze.
4. Final Cause:
   Also known as the purpose or function, this is the reason why something exists or is done. For the statue, the final cause might be to honor a deity, commemorate a person, or simply to beautify a space.

As he did in the rest of his philosophical theories, Aristotle empha-sized the importance of empirical observation in his classification. He meticulously observed and documented different species of living beings, noting their habits, habitats, and anatomical features. This emphasis on observation carries on in modern scientific methods, where classification is often based on extensive data gathering and observable traits. Modern binomial nomenclature (developed by Carl Linnaeus and in which two terms are used to denote a species of living organism) owes much to Ar-istotle's foundations but uses a more detailed hierarchy based on genetic relationships and evolutionary history.

The need to classify and organize information is just as critical in the digital world, especially when dealing with user data. Consider the sheer volume of information you generate during your daily online activities. This includes everything from sending messages and watching videos to writing comments and liking posts. Not only is there a vast amount of activity taking place, but each of these interactions also comes in a wide variety of formats. Combining this high volume and data diversity into a harmonized whole is a task as complex as it is necessary.

To effectively understand the information they possess and to develop strategies for its use, businesses frequently develop a "user data taxon-omy." A taxonomy is essentially a structured classification system that organizes data into categories and subcategories, much like a large cabinet with many drawers. A taxonomy allows for a more efficient analysis and retrieval of specific types of data, which results in faster insights.

Asking the Right Questions

When building a taxonomy, a good idea is to think about your users and ask questions that are progressively more specific to figure out who they are and what they want. This will give you a preliminary pyramid of ques-tions, which may look like this (Figure 4.1).

The lower two stages help understand user profiles not as individu-als but grouped at the segment level, which makes it easier to manage communication. Once that is established, the company can move into looking at what they want and what they need, particularly regarding the products and services offered. At the top of the pyramid sits the key

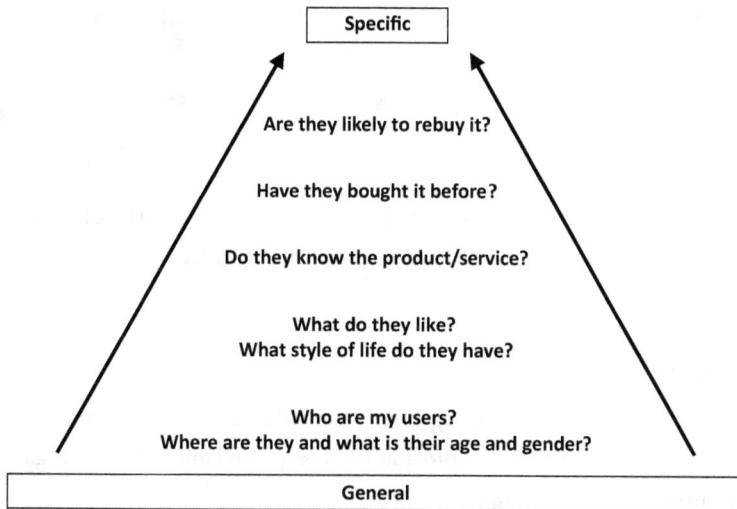

Figure 4.1 For an organization to build its consumer data taxonomy, it must first address some questions about its intended customer audience

question every business wants to answer: Will they buy my product/service? And, will they buy it more than once?

Answering that question is key because conversion is the main metric for business success. In the digital space, conversion is about transforming an online interaction into a desired action. This action could be anything that aligns with the business goals, such as making a purchase, signing up for a newsletter, filling out a contact form, or downloading a resource.

Building the Pyramid

With those questions and answers in mind, we can move into building the actual taxonomy.

This framework can be visualized as a pyramid, where the most basic, foundational information resides at the base, and the data becomes progressively more detailed and nuanced as you move up the pyramid. Tiers within this pyramid, such as "alignment" (which assesses whether a person's values and style align with the brand), "purchase intent" (which indicates whether a person plans to buy a product or service), and "conversion" (which tracks whether a person has completed a purchase), collectively reveal the level of engagement that a particular user segment or group has with the company.

The following steps will guide us through this process:

1. Identify data types:
   The initial step involves identifying the various categories of user data being collected. Common categories include:
   - Demographic data.
   - Behavioral data.
   - Psychographic data.

   By systematically categorizing these data types, businesses can ensure that all relevant information is captured and properly organized from the outset.

2. Establish data hierarchies:
   Data hierarchies involve grouping similar data types into structured levels. For example, within the broader category of demographic data, you might create subcategories such as:
   - Age ranges (e.g., 18 to 24, 25 to 34).
   - Gender (e.g., male, female, nonbinary).
   - Income levels (e.g., low, medium, high).

   Establishing these hierarchical structures allows for granular analysis, enabling companies to "drill down" into specific data points as needed for a deeper understanding.

3. Define data attributes:
   Each category of data should be accompanied by clearly defined attributes that describe the specific characteristics of the data being collected. For instance:

   Psychographic data attributes might include:
   - Lifestyle preferences (e.g., active, homebody).
   - Interests (e.g., sports, music, travel).
   - Values (e.g., sustainability, family, innovation).

   Purchase Data attributes might include:
   - Past purchases, date, price, and product.
   - Abandoned shopping cart items, and the date they were abandoned.

   These attributes provide detailed context and ensure consistency in data interpretation.

4. Standardize data:

   To maintain data consistency and accuracy, it is essential to standardize how data is collected, stored, and labeled. This involves:
   - Establishing consistent naming conventions.
   - Defining data formats (e.g., date formats, currency formats).
   - Implementing data validation rules.

     Standardization ensures that data from diverse sources can be seamlessly integrated and compared, facilitating comprehensive analysis.

5. Create metadata tags:

   Metadata, often described as "data about data," involves attaching descriptive tags to different data sets. These tags provide context and make it easier to retrieve specific data when needed.

     For example:
   - Tagging consumer transaction data with specific purchase dates, product categories, or customer IDs enables efficient analysis of sales trends and customer behavior.
   - Tagging website activity with the source of the traffic, or the campaign that produced the traffic.

Metadata tags improve data discoverability and facilitate more effective data management (Figure 4.2).

The user data taxonomy can take many forms but, ultimately, it is there to serve the objectives and needs of the organization. An automotive company will need to understand the basic characteristics of its prospective customers, like demographics and location, but also look at the data points that influence specific car purchases like fuel economy preferences. An insurance company should be looking at income level as well as financial risk and credit scoring.

Epicurus, Aristotle, and Your Time Online

Whether a for-profit company aims to boost revenue or a nonprofit organization seeks to spread a message, both face a common hurdle: how to create relevant engagement and capture attention in the crowded digital landscape. A purely transactional perspective might advocate

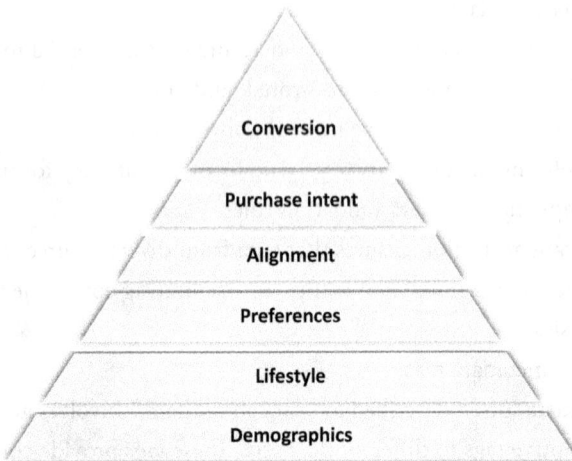

Figure 4.2 *A data taxonomy often takes the shape of a pyramid where the most basic information resides at the base, and the data becomes progressively more detailed and nuanced as you move up*

for indiscriminate data utilization, flooding users with any content imaginable.

However, what Epicurus teaches us about the connection between *ataraxia*, the user experience, and the application of data boils down to the human factor and the intelligent application of Sophia. By genuinely understanding and respecting the nuances in individual preferences, organizations can design interactions that resonate with users, cultivating trust and fostering meaningful engagement.

In this context, user data goes beyond its role as a mere tool for optimization. Instead, it becomes a fundamental component in the endeavor to elevate the digital human experience. It's about using information not just to sell or persuade, but to create a more harmonious online environment, to understand the human on the other side of the screen.

CHAPTER 5

Aporia: Socratic Wisdom to Build Your Digital Plan

Aporia and the Puzzling Journey to Digital Maturity

If we were to believe Plato's writing, Socrates must have been an extremely frustrating interlocutor. And probably a bit of a bully.

Most of what we know about the "first philosopher" comes from the writing that his pupil left. In the Platonic *Dialogues*, a series of philosophical texts, Plato describes his teacher Socrates in conversation with various other characters discussing principles of thought and philosophy. Plato uses this format to explore complex philosophical ideas through discussion. Often, they involve Socrates asking probing questions over and over to challenge assumptions, expose contradictions, and encourage deeper thinking.

One can only imagine what the subject of Socrates's superb dialectic fencing must have felt. Picture some of his interlocutors, Thrasymachus, Gorgias, or Meno, all of them upstanding Athenian citizens, sitting at the meeting grounds of the agora or a banquet listening while Socrates challenged their beliefs and knowledge in public; they may have wriggled in their benches, folding under an incessant barrage of Socratic wit and nervously glancing around as a larger number of onlookers gathered.

Socrates's aim, according to Plato, was to drive the participant to utter confusion and puzzlement as the first step toward gaining true knowledge. The purpose was noble, and it was done for the benefit of the participant as well as the spectators, but it must have been excruciating.

That state of confusion that Socrates aimed for, Plato called *aporia*.

One of the most famous examples of aporia is in Plato's "Meno." In this dialogue, Meno asks Socrates whether virtue can be taught. After the old philosopher asks a series of probing questions, Meno becomes frustrated and confused. He exclaims that Socrates has left him in a state of puzzlement, and he no longer knows what virtue is or whether it can be taught.

Socrates replies that this sense of perplexity is valuable. *Aporia* is not a negative condition but rather the necessary first step toward wisdom and knowledge. The term itself comes from the Greek word "ἀπορία," which literally means "without a path" or "no way out." It is often described as a philosophical impasse, where a person realizes they are stuck, unsure of how to proceed or find their assumptions challenged.

In my professional career, I have met many senior executives in a similar state when discussing digital transformation and the digital sphere. They are certain their organization is in dire need of a digital revamp, but are lost about how to achieve it or what process they have to follow. I often feel that is not an altogether bad thing; in fact, it sounds very similar to what Socrates saw as the necessary first step in the journey.

In Meno, the dialogue further introduces "Meno's Paradox," which is closely tied to the concept of *aporia*. Meno argues that if you don't know what you're looking for, you won't recognize it when you find it, and if you do know, there's no need to search. This paradox suggests that inquiry is impossible.

Socrates counters this paradox with the theory of *anamnesis* (recollection), suggesting that knowledge is already within us, and through questioning and dialogue, we can recall or unearth this buried information and recognize it. This process of recollection is what helps overcome the *aporia* induced by Meno's Paradox.

Again, that is very close to what many decision makers say about their organizations and the need for digitalization and digital innovation. They may not know exactly "what" digitalization means for them or know "how" to implement it but if they see it, they are confident they will recognize it.

Aporia is not merely a state of confusion but a vital part of the learning process. It encourages people to question their assumptions and to dig deeper into problems. Without experiencing doubt or perplexity, one might never engage in true intellectual discovery.

So, how can somebody overcome *aporia* in the digital transformation journey? If you are looking to change your company, where do you start? Well, if one is "without a path," the first thing to do is to use a map to find where you are and where you are going. That is what the digital maturity scale is for.

A digital maturity scale comes in many forms and different stages but, in short, is a tool used to assess an organization's progress in adopting and integrating digital technologies into its operations, strategies, and culture. It helps companies understand their current level of digital transformation and guides them in advancing their digital capabilities to remain competitive.

Here is an example of what the various stages may look like:

1. Initial Stage:
   ○ Characteristics: The use of digital tools is sporadic and uncoordinated. There is no defined strategy for digital transformation.
   ○ Challenges: Lack of digital skills and awareness, resistance to change, and unclear vision.
   ○ Overcoming *aporia*: Begin by identifying the overarching goal and the key digital tools that could enhance basic operations and create small, manageable pilot projects to demonstrate value.
2. Developing Stage:
   ○ Characteristics: There are some digital initiatives in place, but they are not well-integrated. Efforts are mostly isolated within departments, which use outsourced digital tools but not in-house ones.
   ○ Challenges: Fragmentation, inconsistent digital literacy across the organization, and limited cross-functional collaboration.
   ○ Overcoming *aporia*: Establish a culture of digital innovation in the different teams and designate stakeholders for a transformation task force.
3. Defined Stage:
   ○ Characteristics: A clear digital strategy exists, and there is a more coordinated approach to digital initiatives. Efforts are aligned with business goals.
   ○ Challenges: Ensuring alignment across all levels of the organization and securing ongoing buy-in from stakeholders.
   ○ Overcoming *aporia*: Communicate the benefits and progress of the digital strategy and engage with employees at all levels to expand the culture of digital innovation.

4. Managed Stage:
   ○ Characteristics: Digital transformation is integrated into the organization's operations and strategy, with measurable outcomes and key performance indicators (KPIs). Attribution and measurement of digital touchpoints are in place.
   ○ Challenges: Maintaining momentum, managing data effectively, and continuously improving processes.
   ○ Overcoming *aporia*: Invest in training and development to keep digital skills up-to-date and implement a robust data management strategy to support decision making.
5. Optimized Stage:
   ○ Characteristics: The organization is fully connected, continuously improves using digital technologies and is seen as a leader in innovation and digital transformation. There is a "360° user view."
   ○ Challenges: Staying ahead of emerging technologies and maintaining a culture of innovation and agility.
   ○ Overcoming Aporia: Avoid complacency. Foster an environment of continuous learning and experimentation and stay informed about industry trends and technological advancements (Figure 5.1).

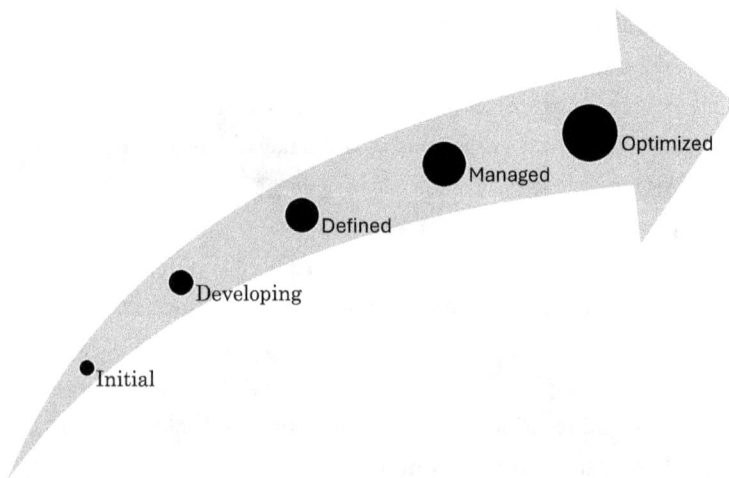

Figure 5.1 There are five stages of increased complexity in the digital maturity scale

Forget Technology and Start with Questions: A Pizza Story

Identifying where the organization falls in this digital maturity scale is useful because it will help to answer the two fundamental questions posed by the process of *aporia*:

1. Where are you?
2. Where are you going?

And to answer these, you need to address five dimensions. These five dimensions show the scope of your digital capabilities and how they map to the digital maturity scale:

1. Audience: Who are you talking to?
   Identify what type of user or consumer you want to address. Organize and leverage data to identify and reach your audience.
2. Message: What do you want to say?
   Define the type of message you want to deliver and how you will do it. What is the call to action for your users?
3. Space: Where will this happen?
   Define your digital properties. Create a platform that is suited to the first two dimensions: audience and message.
4. Measurement: How will this be tracked?
   Measure the impact and results of the digital initiative by tracking things like consumer engagement and sales impact, in an attribution-based, data-driven manner.
5. Scale: How will it change?
   Automate marketing and operational processes to streamline efficiency and improve scalability. The system must be future-proofed to assure continuity (Figure 5.2).

If you are looking for a powerful story in digital transformation and on how to ask the right questions to create innovation, look no further than pizza.

In the early 2000s, the U.S. company Domino's Pizza faced declining sales and a poor brand reputation due to product quality concerns.

QUESTIONS	DIMENSIONS	MATURITY STAGE

01
Audience

02
Message

1
Where are you?

03
Space

04
Measurement

2
Where are you going?

05
Scale

- Optimized
- Managed
- Defined
- Developing
- Initial

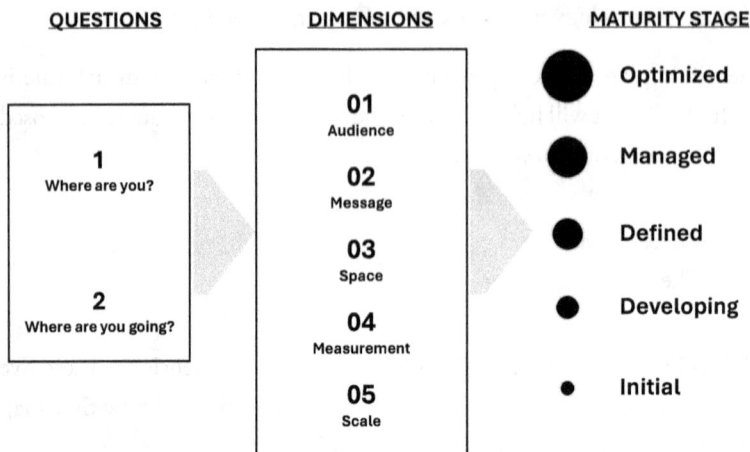

Figure 5.2 Identifying the correct stage in the digital maturity scale requires asking two questions and addressing five different dimensions

Business was not good, and neither was the morale of the leadership team and employees. Patrick Doyle, who served as the company's CEO from 2010 to 2018, may not have been a digital expert, but he understood early on that the key to overcoming their problems was to embark on a full-scale transformation, heavily leveraging digital technology.

We knew that to succeed, we had to change more than the pizza. We needed to change the entire way we interact with our customers, and technology was the answer.

That is what they did. Under Doyle's leadership, Domino's underwent a major overhaul in both its product quality and business model, with a particular focus on digital innovation. Domino's wanted to understand its customers and reshape the entire pizza ordering experience so the company introduced the "Domino's AnyWare" platform, which allowed customers to order pizza via various digital channels such as smartphones, smart TVs, smartwatches, and even voice assistants like Amazon's Alexa. They made it so easy that you didn't even have to type the word "pizza," you could just tweet a pizza emoji. And to make the user experience as smooth as possible, they removed stages in the ordering process launching the "Zero-Click" ordering app where customers could simply open the app and let it count down to zero for the order to be placed automatically.

By 2020, Domino's stock had increased more than 2,000 percent over the previous decade and outperformed other restaurant brands, positioning itself as a digital leader in the food delivery industry. By 2021, over 75 percent of Domino's orders in the United States were coming through digital channels. But the company was modernizing also on the back end by implementing digital systems to optimize supply chain management, reduce waste, and manage inventory more effectively. They used data analytics to predict demand in real time and ensure the right resources were in place at each location.

As important as all the technical tools were, the biggest transformation was in the company's mindset. Domino's nurtured an internal culture of innovation by blending technology with traditional processes. It invested in tech talent, set up digital labs, and focused on digital marketing, online sales, and improving the customer interface.

Central to this narrative is how Domino's Pizza halted its decline, confronted a phase of *aporia*, and emerged successfully by answering two fundamental questions: Who are we? And where do we want to go? Their answer: "We are a pizza company, and we want to become the easiest place on Earth to order pizza."

Crafting the Plan

After measuring where you are in the digitalization maturity scale, the real work starts. It is time to draft your digital transformation plan. Here again, there are questions to be answered (Figure 5.3).

Answering each of these questions will help you build a fully-fledged digital transformation strategy. In each question, there is a set of tasks you need to address (Figure 5.4).

1. Where Do You Want to Go?

Competitive Analysis:

The first step in understanding where you want to go should be to look at the competition and see what they are doing.

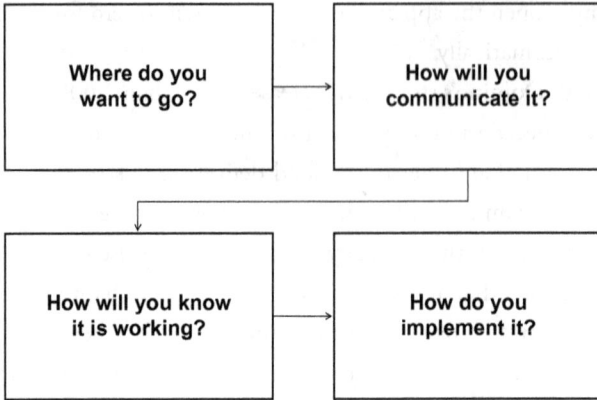

Figure 5.3 *In order to craft a digital transformation plan, the organization needs to answer four specific questions*

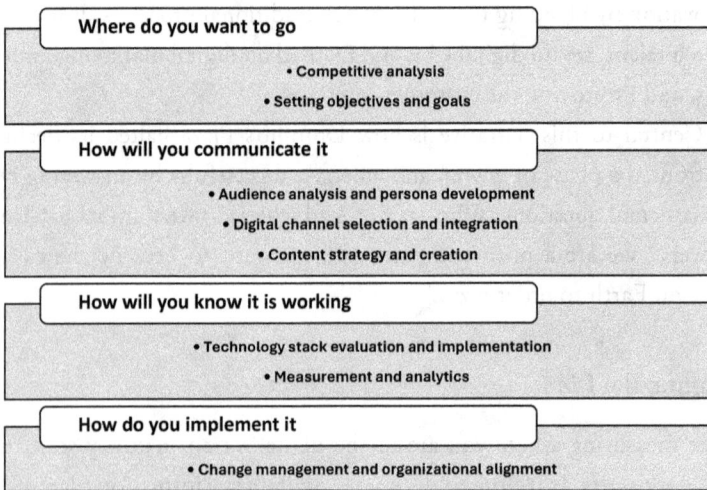

Figure 5.4 *For each question, the organizations need to address a set of tasks to build their digital transformation plan*

Start by identifying key competitors. Study both established and emerging companies in your industry and see what changes they are implementing, either digital or not. Visit their websites, social media strategies, and look at what content they post. Try to identify their customer engagement techniques.

Be critical about it, determine where competitors are excelling and where there might be opportunities for differentiation. If you see a gap or an opening, ask how your company can exploit that to take the lead in that field.

Airbnb disrupted the traditional hotel industry by leveraging a digital-first strategy. Unlike many established hotel chains, which focused on in-person services and real estate, Airbnb capitalized on the concept of the "gig economy" and put digital platforms in place to connect offer and demand. They used data-driven competitive analysis to offer users unique accommodations, a frictionless interface for the booking process, and a personalized user experience.

Setting Objectives and Goals:

A successful digital strategy is not a standalone entity. It must be a direct extension of your overall business strategy. When your business aims to expand into new markets, for instance, your digital approach should mirror that ambition through localization, targeted advertising, and perhaps even a mobile-first approach for reaching global customers. A frequent pitfall is treating digital efforts as a separate venture with disconnected goals.

Consider McDonald's digital transformation. Their strategy was meticulously aligned with their core business objectives: enhancing customer experience and driving growth. They implemented self-service kiosks, a user-friendly mobile app, and engaging digital loyalty programs. These initiatives streamlined the ordering and payment process, making it more convenient for customers. This, in turn, resulted in increased sales.

If you are not clear how to set up these objectives, use the SMART framework:

- Specific: Define what exactly you want to achieve.
- Measurable: Quantify your objectives.
- Achievable: Ensure the goals are realistic based on current capabilities.
- Relevant: Align the objectives with business priorities.
- Time-bound: Set a clear timeline to track progress.

2. How Will You Communicate It?

Audience Analysis and Persona Development:

Once you know what you want to do and what other companies are doing, you should turn your attention to the most important player in the ecosystem: The user. Same as Domino's Pizza did, ask yourself the following question, "What do consumer wants from us? What is the value we can provide?" Maybe they want an easier, faster way of ordering pizza with minimum hurdles. Maybe they want to watch a movie on their digital devices without lag and in high-resolution. Or they may want a way to effortlessly test a new car before they buy it. All these needs can be addressed using digital technology, but the key issue is figuring out the audience you are addressing and tailoring your digital strategies to the right user segments.

Effective audience analysis involves gathering data on customer demographics, behavior, preferences, and pain points. Companies like Spotify or Booking.com do this through their rich data collection on user habits (music, travel preferences, etc.), which helps the company segment its users and deliver recommendations.

If you want to go even further, you can create detailed *personas*. These are avatars of the different audience segments, making it easier to visualize and understand them. Amazon has created personas for different user groups, enabling highly targeted advertising and content.

Failing to understand your consumer will result in consumer dissatisfaction. When Yahoo was the dominant search engine company in the early 2000s, it failed to effectively target its audience segments in the same way the up-and-coming Google was doing. While Google refined its search algorithms to cater to different users' personas, Yahoo's unfocused approach led to a decline in consumer satisfaction, resulting in a substantial loss of market share.

Digital Channel Selection and Integration:

Defining who you plan to address and who your audience is will help your company select the best channels to communicate with them. Selecting and integrating the right digital channels is a key step to maximize the effectiveness of your digital strategy and meet your customers where they already are. Cosmetic retailer Sephora excels in this area by combining a brick-and-mortar experience with a robust online presence. Customers can seamlessly transition between the in-store and digital experiences through their mobile app, loyalty program, and online store.

And if you plan to use multiple digital channels (social media, apps, websites, online advertising, etc.) they must be properly integrated, so users receive a consistent brand experience all across. Disney does this by using the "My Disney Experience" platform, where customers can plan their visits, book rides, and access special offers across mobile and desktop.

Content Strategy and Creation:

Once you know who you will be speaking with and where, then you need to define the message. User attention is the scarcest and most valuable currency in the digital ecosystem. Every second, a myriad of companies, organizations, content creators and individuals push their content into the digital universe, but it is only valuable if somebody is there to receive it.

Because of the difficulty of attracting and holding attention, your content should be relevant and engaging. Everything you put out there has to be built around the needs and preferences of your audience and focus on delivering value at every stage of the user journey. Ads are just one format for content, but others like blog posts, whitepapers, and webinars are also valuable.

Some companies become known for their unorthodox communication strategy. Beverage manufacturer Red Bull, for example, has built a global brand around content creation that does not rely on direct messaging or advertising but rather sponsoring events and associating the brand with life experiences that resonate with its target audience

3. How Will You Know It's Working?

Technology Stack Evaluation and Implementation:

As important as planning, goals, cultural changes, and user analysis are, at the end of the day, any digital transformation process relies on a layer of technology to make it work. There is no shortage of vendors out there, so this technology stack or technological infrastructure can take many forms; the task during this planning stage is to evaluate the current technology the company is using and identify deficiencies.

After that, choosing appropriate tools, such as CRM, and analytics systems, is a matter of selection. Salesforce has become the gold standard in sales and consumer management platforms that are highly scalable.

Measurement and Analytics:

Tracking performance is essential to understanding whether your digital strategy is working.

Although digital strategy shares the same business goals as the company, its performance metrics will be different. KPIs in digital transformation are related to how well you engage the user and the level of their response. These include conversion rates, website traffic, bounce rates, click-through rates for calls to action, and so on. Businesses like music platform Spotify track tailor-made metrics such as time spent listening, churn rates, and engagement on its premium service to understand how well the platform is working.

All these metrics are tracked via analytics tools which translate the raw data into insights.

4. How Do You Implement It?

Change Management and Organizational Alignment:

Even the most meticulous planning and advanced technological infrastructure will prove ineffective if an organization fails to implement internal changes at the same speed. Digitalization, by its very nature, introduces disruption, and disruption causes a shift in the balance of internal working methods. Some divisions, such as traditional IT services, manual data entry, or certain aspects of the sales process, may be diminished or even eliminated. Conversely, areas like data management and customer relations will rise in priority. Teams, tools, flows, and so on are all upended when data and the meticulous tracking of user touchpoints suddenly become a focus. People need to learn and adapt to the new digital reality, and that requires effort.

Values such as openness to change and a willingness to embrace innovation must be communicated clearly and consistently throughout the group, which ensures that every level, from top management to frontline employees, understands and actively supports the transformation.

Successful digital transformation hinges on engaging stakeholders from various functions. This means involving not only top leadership but also tech teams, operational managers, customer service representatives, and other relevant departments. Engaging these stakeholders early and continuously ensures that everyone is aligned and understands their role in its implementation. For example, General Electric's digital transformation was driven by a companywide approach that included key players from leadership, IT, and operations. This collaborative effort enabled the company to better integrate digital tools and processes into its core operations.

Implementing structured change management practices is crucial to overcoming resistance and fostering acceptance. Microsoft's transformation under CEO Satya Nadella is a prime example. By shifting to a "learn-it-all" culture, Microsoft moved from a traditional software model to a cloud-first, mobile-first company. Nadella emphasized cultural transformation through upskilling, continuous learning, and openness to new ideas, allowing the organization to adapt successfully to the digital-first strategy.

Be Ready for Failure

One thing to remember when planning the digital transformation process is that not everything will go well. An important part of the effort is about testing new things so that, by studying successes and failures, organizations can better navigate the process. Understanding why certain strategies succeeded while others faltered informs future digital initiatives. A company that is willing to test and try, that moves nimbly and anticipates challenges, refines its strategies and implements adjustments will come through in a better place.

Aporia and Beyond

Imagine you are sitting in front of Socrates, back in the Athens of the classical period. You tell the stern philosopher about your intention to take your company or organization through a digital transformation process. What questions do you think he would ask? Most certainly, there would be at least two: What is digital transformation is and why do you think you need it?

Would you be able to answer, especially as he probes more and more to test your understanding?

Socrates may not be here, but those questions still need addressing. Embracing *aporia* is not merely an intellectual exercise but a vital and transformative phase in the journey toward digital maturity. Just as Socrates wielded confusion as a tool for enlightenment, organizations can pressure-test the assumptions and goals of their digitalization ideas to catalyze substantial growth and innovation.

That initial state of confusion, of being "without a path," is not a stumbling block but a gateway to deeper understanding. Leaders often feel lost in the vast landscape of digital transformation, grappling with uncharted territories of technology, consumer behavior, and market demands. Yet, as demonstrated by the cases of Domino's, the journey through this complexity can yield powerful results.

Recalling the two fundamental questions we started with, we can now see how to address them.

- Where are you?
  Use the digital maturity scale to answer this. This scale serves as a comprehensive map, illustrating an organization's current position in its digital journey.
- Where are you going?
  Build a well-defined digital transformation plan to answer this. This plan acts as a detailed blueprint, outlining the specific actions and strategies required to reach the desired digital destination.

Together, these tools—the digital maturity scale and the digital transformation plan—not only guide organizations to a successful digital future, but also equip them to innovate confidently and boldly in a constantly changing digital landscape.

Just as Socrates intended.

CHAPTER 6

Aristotle's Rhetoric: The Art and Science of Digital Marketing

Aristotle's Rhetoric and the Art of the Digital Marketer

Socrates and Plato loom large in the history of philosophy, but Aristotle is an equally impressive figure. A gifted polymath, he studied under Plato at the Athenian academy for almost 20 years and, after his teacher's death, was hired by the Macedonian king Philip II to tutor his son Alexander, the man who history will later know as "The Great."

Aristotle was a revolutionary thinker who didn't accept inherited wisdom at face value. Here is a good example: At a time when the common theory was that the Earth was flat, Aristotle was among the first to recognize that our planet was actually a round sphere. When he came out with the idea, it was received with general skepticism by the people of ancient Greece, so Aristotle explained to his audience that one of the clearest indications of a curved Earth is how the night sky changes as one moves north or south. He pointed out that when travelers journey south toward Egypt, certain constellations that were not visible in Greece would begin to appear above the horizon. Conversely, when travelers moved north toward Thrace, other constellations would disappear from view. This wasn't merely an occasional occurrence but a consistent and predictable change in the night sky, experienced by sailors and traders over long distances.

"Imagine," he told the audience.

You are standing at the edge of a hill and watching someone descend into a valley. As they go further down, the lower part of their body disappears first, followed by the upper part, until they are no longer visible. This is the same effect we see with the stars when traveling across great distances on Earth.

Aristotle reasoned that this phenomenon could only be explained by a curved surface. If the Earth were flat, the same constellations would be visible everywhere, regardless of how far north or south one was.

Aristotle was a logical thinker, and he applied deductive methodology to everything he did. His main philosophical development was that of the rhetoric, the art of persuasion, which he envisioned as a counterpart to dialectic, the prevalent Socratic method of inquiry and discussion between two people (often in the form of a dialogue) used by his teacher Plato as a tool to achieve wisdom.

Just as modern advertisers and marketers, Aristotle had a shrewd understanding of human nature, and he knew people react not only to logic but also to emotion. The rhetoric process he developed involved three modes of appeal:

1. Ethos (credibility):
   Ethos refers to the credibility or character of the speaker. Aristotle explained to his students that people trust those with authority or expertise, and establishing *ethos* helps build this initial trust.
2. Pathos (emotion):
   Pathos refers to the appeal to emotions, designed to elicit feelings like joy, anger, fear, or sympathy to persuade the audience. Aristotle emphasized that the appeal to emotion stirs hearts and grabs attention, moving people closer to making a decision.
3. Logos (logic):
   Logos is the appeal to logic and reason, emphasizing evidence, facts, and logical arguments to persuade the audience.

Anyone who has been online would recognize the elements of Aristotle's rhetoric in the interaction between brands, advertisers, and their audiences.

- Influencers in social media who make tangents to talk about a particular product are leveraging their credibility, their *ethos*, to build a trust bridge between themselves, the consumer and the product. Advertisers utilize a range of tactics to establish credibility when they seek expert endorsements, feature third-party reviews, and obtain quality certifications. Brands invest significant resources to build *ethos* via blogs, white papers, and videos, all designed to position themselves as thought leaders and demonstrate their expertise.

- Emotional appeal is a core strategy in digital advertising, where *pathos* is used to evoke responses that drive user engagement, clicks, and conversions. Watch any social media feed or video ad and you will notice they apply compelling visuals and moving narratives. For example, a heartfelt video about a charitable cause can drive donations by tapping into viewers' sense of empathy. Alternatively, advertisers may leverage urgency and scarcity to create a sense of the fear of missing out (FOMO) using countdown timers, limited-time offers, or stock limitations, all strategically designed to encourage users to act swiftly by triggering an emotional response. Consumer product brands are particularly adept at cultivating relatability. They incorporate memes, playful GIFs, and witty copy into their content on platforms like X or Instagram, creating a sense of delight to appear more approachable and human. This emotional connection fosters a stronger bond with consumers, driving engagement and loyalty.

- Regarding logic or *logos*, all advertising leverages factual product features, benefits, or specifications, especially in industries like technology, finance, or health care. This approach appeals to the logical side of consumers, emphasizing why a product is the best choice based on measurable attributes. In business-to-business advertising (content aimed at corporate buyers), the emphasis on *logos* is even more pronounced. Companies frequently disseminate white papers, informative infographics, and detailed case studies to provide logical evidence of a product or service's effectiveness. Presenting concrete statistics, ROI metrics, and other quantifiable data directly engages the rational mind of corporate decision makers, fostering trust and driving informed purchasing decisions.

Successful digital advertising often blends all three elements (*ethos*, *pathos*, and *logos*) to create well-rounded campaigns.

- *Ethos + Pathos*: An influencer campaign builds credibility (*ethos*) while simultaneously telling an inspiring story (*pathos*) to connect emotionally.
- *Pathos + Logos*: A retargeting ad uses an urgent emotional appeal (*pathos*) while presenting logical evidence, such as discounts or customer testimonials (*logos*), to reinforce the message.
- *Ethos + Logos*: A LinkedIn ad promoting a professional service emphasizes credentials (*ethos*) and case studies with quantifiable results (*logos*) to attract rational buyers.

As you may have noticed, a key premise of this book is the enduring nature of human psychology. Despite the passage of millennia, certain fundamental aspects of our mental processes remain remarkably consistent. One of the most prominent examples is the desire to influence people's interests and guide their choices in a particular direction.

Modern advertising agencies, marketers, and brands rely on the same mental mechanisms that Aristotle established in his rhetoric. His work serves as a foundational framework for understanding the pulls and levers behind ad persuasion, enabling advertisers to craft digital campaigns that resonate deeply with their target audiences. It is via *ethos*, *pathos*, and *logos* that Apple. Coca-Cola, Ford, and many others speak to all of us, day in and day out, broadcasting messages that attract our attention.

The Evolution of Marketing:
From Mad Men to Online Ads

What we call the "digital marketing ecosystem" is a complex space that encompasses all the tools, platforms, strategies, and processes that businesses use to engage with customers online. It is a dazzling and evolving landscape full of technologies that requires a clear understanding of its components and dynamics if one is to drive growth, satisfy users, and leverage data effectively. It is also one of the fundamental pillars for any company looking to transform digitally because marketing can be considered the main monetization engine of the online world; the one thing that bankrolls everything else.

Marketing has always been complex because, same as Aristotle's rhetoric, its core objective is to persuade people who may not be receptive to your message. However, the marketing landscape has experienced a profound transformation in recent decades. This evolution has shifted the focus from traditional, broad-reach media, such as television and print, to highly targeted and interactive digital channels. Understanding this evolution (from the mass-market approaches of traditional marketing to the personalized, data-driven strategies of digital marketing) is essential for appreciating the significant advantages of today's dynamic digital marketing ecosystem. The core principles of persuasion that Aristotle wrote about are now applied in a completely different way.

Traditional marketing has been a foundational element of business promotion. Its approach centers on using broad media channels to reach a vast audience. Typically, this involves minimal segmentation and targeting, meaning that same message is delivered to a wide range of individuals, without significant customization.

- Television is the main and most complex broad media channel. It combines audio and visual elements to create compelling advertisements that generate strong emotional responses. However, TV ads are typically expensive, and their effectiveness is often measured through broad metrics like viewership ratings rather than direct engagement or conversion rates.
- Print media includes newspapers, magazines, brochures, and other printed materials. While print ads can deliver detailed information and have a longer lifespan (e.g., magazines can be stored for months), they struggle with real-time updates and lack interactivity. Because they can be quite specialized, they offer a degree of credibility, especially for certain industries like automotive and luxury goods, but measuring their impact is challenging.
- Radio provides another form of broad media marketing, offering local, regional and national reach through audio-based advertisements. It is cost-effective and flexible, allowing for localized messaging. Radio ads are effective for building awareness, especially

during commuting hours, but they lack visual elements and are typically short, which limits the depth of the message.

- Outdoor advertising, such as billboards, transit ads, and posters, remains a popular way to reach a wide audience. It is highly visible and has the potential to make a significant impact through repetition. However, it lacks personalization, interactivity, and precise targeting, making it less suitable for niche products or services.

The golden age of traditional marketing is often exemplified by the *Mad Men* TV show, a drama series that ran from 2007 to 2015 on cable network AMC. The show, same as the actual industry of the period, focused on the work of advertising agencies that worked on creating impactful campaigns for mass audiences. This period prioritized crafting compelling storytelling and emotional appeal, with companies relying on catchy slogans (developed largely without direct audience feedback) to capture the public's imagination. Marketers relied heavily on intuition, creativity, and broad demographic data to guide their strategies. The success of a campaign was evaluated mainly by reach, brand recall, and general market share.

That all changed with the advent of the Internet and digital technology. If there is one key difference between the *Mad Men* era of advertising and the brave new world that technology brought, it is the communication shift from a monologue to a dialogue between advertisers and their audience. The moment that technology made it possible for consumers to convey their opinion in real time via highly visible comments, actions or reviews, marketing changed, and the balance of power shifted with it.

Up until that moment, brands and advertisers had broadcast their message into the void and waited with crossed fingers to see a spike in sales. They would then tweak their message and repeat the process. Anybody who wanted more specific data could set up consumer panels to find the voice of the buyer and adjust their offering accordingly.

Unlike broad media approaches, digital marketing allows for granular targeting, real-time performance tracking, and interactive engagement with audiences. The shift to digital marketing redefined key marketing parameters:

- Reach: Traditional marketing, with its limited range of available channels, could only aim for broad reach, often based on basic demographics. A car manufacturer may advertise in a news program to try and reach potential customers, or a cosmetic company may advertise in a lifestyle magazine, but the impact on truly potential customers was very hard to gauge. Digital technology has created a myriad of new channels like websites, blogs, social media accounts, and YouTube channels, and this, in turn, allows for both broad and highly targeted reach. Marketers can now identify specific audience segments based on demographics, behaviors, interests, and even real-time location. Where traditional campaigns were set once launched, digital campaigns can be adjusted on the fly to optimize for better performance.

- Personalization: Digital marketing thrives on personalized experiences and marketers can tailor content, offers, and advertisements to individual users. For instance, e-mail marketing can address users by name and recommend products based on their purchase history, while programmatic advertising (using advertising technology to buy and sell ads) can serve ads relevant to users' recent online actions.

- Content variety: Traditional marketing primarily relied on static content formats like print ads, TV commercials, and radio spots. Digital marketing, on the other hand, offers diverse content formats, including text, video, audio, infographics, interactive ads, and user-generated content. This variety enables marketers to create more engaging, informative, and entertaining experiences.

- Monetization: While traditional marketing primarily used cost-per-placement models, where the advertiser pays a fixed amount for ad space, digital marketing allows for multiple revenue models, creating a flexible approach to monetization. For example:
  - Cost-per-Click (CPC): Advertisers pay only when a user clicks on an ad, making this model highly performance-driven.
  - Cost-per-Impression (CPM): Advertisers pay per thousand impressions, ensuring that their brand reaches a large audience.

○ Cost-per-Action (CPA): Advertisers pay when a user completes a desired action, such as making a purchase or filling out a form.

Not Better, Just Different (But Also Better)

Is digital marketing inherently better than traditional media marketing? Not necessarily, although there is a technology and communication system evolution at play, each type of media plays a particular role. Online newspapers may be quite convenient, but many readers would always prefer the feel of reading on paper. Online video platforms cover very specific areas of interest not supported by linear or digital TV broadcasters, but a large segment of the audience still prefers the production values present in broadcasted programs.

That said, from a marketing point of view, there are some key advantages to running digital media campaigns versus those possible in traditional media.

- Real-time data and analytics: Digital marketing allows marketers to access real-time data and analytics to get insights into campaign performance so they can refine strategies quickly and make data-driven decisions.
- Greater targeting precision: Digital marketing leverages sophisticated targeting algorithms to deliver messages to the right audiences at the right time.
- Higher engagement levels: Digital marketing facilitates interactive engagement through social media, comments, likes, shares, and direct messaging. It allows two-way communication, creating opportunities for brands to build deeper relationships with their audience.
- Cost-effectiveness: Digital marketing is often more cost-effective, especially for small- and medium-sized businesses. Campaigns can be scaled according to budget, and the effectiveness of each dollar spent can be measured accurately. Traditional marketing often requires significant upfront investment, with results that are harder to measure.

For a company looking to go through a digital transformation process, understanding the way that digital marketing works is key, but traditional marketing still holds value, particularly for building brand awareness and credibility. Many successful campaigns today integrate traditional and digital elements to create an omnichannel experience. A TV ad campaign might direct viewers to a website or social media channel for more information, while print ads might include QR codes to facilitate digital engagement.

Who Pays for All Those Cat Videos?

In ancient Greece, graffiti and inscriptions served as a unique, cost-effective way for merchants to communicate with the public. These writings were placed in prominent locations where people frequently passed by, like walls in the marketplace of the agora, temples, and public buildings.

A merchant selling high-quality olive oil, for instance, might have engraved "Fine oil available here," on stone slabs or walls near the town square. Beyond basic product announcements, early marketers also understood the power of persuasive language and engaging content. Messages might have included personal endorsements, highlighting the quality and value of their products. Humor was another tool, with phrases like, "Buy my wine; it's better than Dionysus's!" designed to pique interest. Similarly, directional messages like, "Excellent leather goods this way," accompanied by an arrow, guided potential customers toward specific locations.

Public criers, or *kērukes*, were also used similarly to modern advertising, verbally announcing everything from sales to local events. Merchants often paid criers to announce special deals, new stock, or market events. On market days, criers were responsible for calling attention to various shops and goods available in the agora. They provided directions, named specific merchants, and used enticing phrases like "three amphorae for the price of two!" to attract larger crowds.

The days of the handwritten slogans and public criers are gone, but the economic model at the heart of advertising is very simple and has not changed much since the classic Greek period. Some people (advertisers) invest time and resources in crafting messages. Their goal is to connect with other people (the audience) who they believe will be interested in their products or services. This basic dynamic of message creation and targeted communication remains unchanged. Advertisers still seek out locations where their messages will achieve maximum visibility. The entities that own or control these spaces (publishers) may charge a fee for the privilege of displaying the message.

The one thing digital advertising has added to this process is scale and complexity.

Doug Weaver is the founder of the Upstream Group and was part of the team that sold the first dozen or so ads on the web (on October 24, 1994, for *WIRED* magazine's *Hot Wired* site). Currently a digital analyst and public speaker, he summarizes the difference between digital media and every other type of marketing channel that has come before. Digital media is an advertising medium where there is virtually no limit to the volume of ad space that can be put up for sale. This is its great advantage but also the source of its inherent complexity.

Advertising "inventory" refers to the number of content units that a publisher has available to sell to an advertiser. In traditional mass media, inventory is determined by space. Whether it is copies and pages in a printed newspaper or magazines, or time on a radio or TV program, the inventory that can be assigned to advertising content is limited and finite. A newspaper has only so many pages, a TV program only so many minutes.

The technology that makes digital marketing possible broke down this barrier. In digital media, the publisher prepares a set of content and makes it available to the users by publishing it on a website, a platform, an app, and so on. Now (and this is the key thing to understand), a copy of the content doesn't exist until the user takes an action like opening the website in a browser, accessing the platform, or logging in to the app. This means that, as opposed to traditional mass media, digital channels have a virtually endless number of copies they can generate, it just depends on how many users decide to access the content. What's more, while mass media must generate the same set of content for all members of the audience (hence the name "mass"), in digital media, each copy of inventory can change content according to the profile of the person who is accessing it.

There is, however, one challenge that pioneers of the digital advertising business could not overcome: how to optimize the sale of digital ad space. Initially, e-publishers followed the traditional, well-tested process used for newspapers and TV: direct sales teams. A salesperson would contact advertisers and agencies and offer to place an ad creative at a certain cost. Prices will vary according to visibility and the estimated number of visitors to the website.

But since the number of ad spaces available for sale was related to the number of page views, accurate planning was nearly impossible. Imagine a YouTube video that goes viral. Regular videos for the same creator may have a few thousand views each day, but if one of the clips connects with the audience, the number of views could increase 10-fold. So, publishers realized that, after selling directly to some advertisers, they often ended up with a portion of leftover unfilled ad inventory. A new solution in the form of ad networks came to be as a way to aggregate this unused inventory. A group of publishers would pool together all their unused ad space to gain scale and offer it to advertisers as a one-stop solution for them to get more reach. Unfortunately, one of the effects of the ad network was that ad space was aggregated simply based on availability and the context or nature of the channel was not always taken into account. Some advertisers were unhappy to see that their brands were being announced in websites of mature, violent or grotesque content.

Also, because of the large number of publishers involved in the process, advertising in digital media either via direct purchase or via ad networks was very labor-intensive, and some kind of automation was required. In 2008, the digital industry got its wish granted and the Ad-Tech (advertising technology) space was born. This automation, although necessary, brought yet another unprecedented level of complexity to the whole online advertising process.

The date is not coincidental; the financial crisis that shocked Wall Street around 2008 left out of work a large number of stock market system engineers and entrepreneurs who turned their hungry gaze to the increasingly rich digital ad industry. Looking to increase the effectiveness of the ad purchase process, they devised a new approach inspired by their financial sector backgrounds. What if advertisers could proactively choose the ad exchange inventory and pay based on the value that they considered it to be worth?

Taking a cue from the stock market, a new system called real-time bidding (RTB) allowed publishers to put their inventory in an ad exchange, a neutral trading ground for buying and selling ad space instead of giving it to an ad network. Advertisers would bid for the best ad location, which would go to the highest paying bidder. Specialized technology companies were set at each end (DSP or demand-side platform on the advertiser end, and SSP or supply-side platform on the publisher end) to regulate the new auctionlike process.

The "real time" part of the name comes from the process itself. In the milliseconds that it takes for a user to open a new page, this freshly created ad space is presented to the advertisers in the ad exchange and, based on bidding prices set by each company according to their interest, it is assigned to the highest paying client. This digital economic model is the foundation of today's marketing ecosystem online, and drives the flow of ads and transactions in a highly efficient way.

As a result, digital advertising is a structured ecosystem where the following players work together to maximize investment and return while leveraging the basic building attributes of the digital sphere (data, measurement, personalization, attribution, etc.):

Advertisers

Advertisers are the brands, agencies, and businesses that create marketing campaigns aimed at promoting their products or services to target audiences. Advertisers are the engine of the digital marketing machine and the primary source of revenue, investing in various channels to achieve brand awareness, lead generation, and sales conversion.

Publishers and Media Channels

Publishers and media are the digital platforms where advertisements are displayed. These include websites, social media platforms, video channels, apps, and other digital properties where users interact with content. Media channels provide the ad inventory, which is the available space or opportunities for displaying advertisements to users.

Technology Platforms

Tech platforms are the intermediaries that make the process between publishers and advertisers possible. They offer technology stacks that facilitate the buying, selling, and optimization of advertising. Some key types of tech platforms are:

- Ad Exchanges: Digital marketplaces that connect advertisers with media owners, enabling the real-time buying and selling of ad inventory.
- Demand-Side Platforms (DSPs): Used by advertisers to automate the buying of ad space based on targeting criteria like audience segments, geographic locations, and interests.
- Supply-Side Platforms (SSPs): Used by media owners to manage and sell their ad inventory online.
- Data Management Platforms (DMPs): Platforms that store and analyze data to help advertisers make more informed targeting decisions.
- Data Providers: Companies that supply user data, helping advertisers refine their targeting strategies and personalize ad content. Data providers collect and distribute all the types of information we saw in the taxonomy building chapter.

The movement of data and money between these different players is highly automated and data-driven. While the underlying mechanics are complex, involving sophisticated algorithms, the fundamental flow looks like this (Figure 6.1).

This process we call programmatic advertising.

The Many Faces of Digital Advertising: Digital Marketing Formats

Imagine you are the CEO of an innovative consumer product company. When planning your digital marketing strategy, every decision you make comes down to investment, return, and risk. You have a limited amount of money to invest in promoting your product. You also have what may seem like an endless number of channels, formats, and places where you can put that money.

ADVERTISER	TECH PLATFORM	PUBLISHER

1-PUBLISHERS
generate ad inventory on their digital properties
making it available through ad exchanges and **SSPs**

2-ADVERTISERS
use **DSPs** to bid for this inventory in real-time
auctions to secure ad space and target audiences

3-DATA
play a critical role in enhancing ad relevance and personalization.
They flow from data providers to **DMPs,** which integrate it with ad
exchanges, DSPs, and SSPs.

4-ADS
are served to users

5-FINANCIAL TRANSACTIONS
occur as advertisers bid for ad space and pay for ad impressions, clicks, or other specified
metrics. These transactions are governed by various **monetization models,** defined by
the publishers.

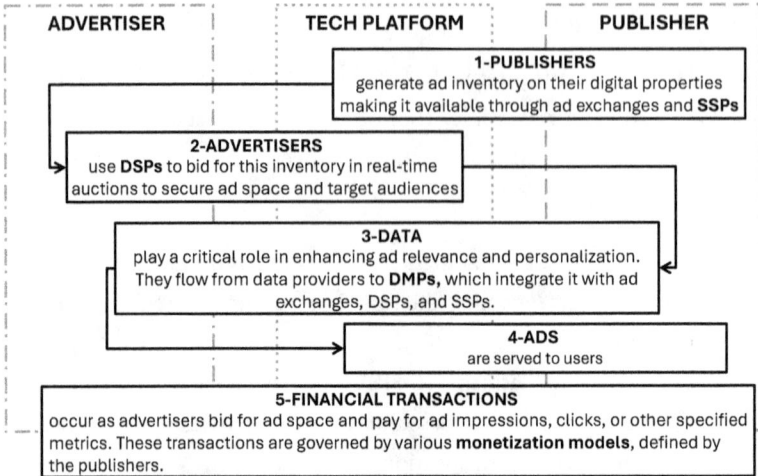

*Figure 6.1 The flow of data and revenue between the different
players in the programmatic advertising process is represented here*

Understanding the various formats of online marketing is crucial for
building a well-rounded campaign because each format offers unique
ways to reach and engage audiences.

Programmatic Marketing

This is the complex process we just discussed. Programmatic advertising
automates the buying and selling of ad placements across digital platforms. It leverages real-time bidding (RTB) to optimize performance
based on user profiles.

A travel agency might use programmatic advertising to reach potential customers who have recently searched for flight deals or visited travel
blogs. By analyzing that data, the agency can serve targeted ads during the
window of opportunity when users are likely to convert.

The industry is quite dynamic, and as digital marketing evolves, new
formats and strategies are emerging, driven by advancements in technology and changing user preferences:

- AI-Powered advertising: AI enables more sophisticated targeting
  and creative optimization. AI-powered tools can analyze large volumes of data to predict user behavior with enhanced precision.

- Contextual targeting: Ads are placed not based on audience profiles but on content aligned with user interests. An ad for hiking gear might appear on an outdoor adventure blog, reaching an audience already interested in outdoor activities. Contextual targeting complies well with privacy regulations because it is not reliant on personal data and has become increasingly relevant.

- Immersive ad formats: Immersive advertising formats such as augmented reality (AR), virtual reality (VR), and interactive ads are gaining popularity. These formats provide users with a type of experience beyond image or video ads.

- Connected TV (CTV) advertising: Connected TV advertising reaches viewers on streaming platforms like Hulu, YouTube TV, and other over-the-top (OTT) devices, such as smart TVs. It combines the power of TV ads and online marketing so brands can target based on viewing preferences and demographics, making CTV an effective way to reach cord-cutting audiences.

Search Marketing

Search marketing focuses on increasing a brand's visibility on search engines like Google and Bing. It consists of two primary strategies: search engine optimization and paid search ads.

- Search Engine Optimization (SEO): SEO involves optimizing a website's content and structure to rank higher in search engine results pages (SERPs). By using keywords, enhancing user experience, and gaining quality backlinks, companies can attract organic (nonpaid) traffic. For instance, a company selling eco-friendly products might optimize its site with keywords like "sustainable living tips" and "eco-friendly products" to attract environmentally conscious consumers searching for these terms.

- Paid Search Ads: Paid search, also known as pay-per-click (PPC) advertising, allows businesses to bid on keywords related to their offerings. Ads appear at the top of SERPs, making them highly visible. For example, an online pet supplies store could bid on keywords like "best dog food" to ensure its ads appear when users search for pet products. Paid search offers immediate visibility and can drive targeted traffic to a website, especially useful for new businesses looking to build a quick online presence.

Social Media Marketing

Social media marketing involves promoting content and interacting with users on platforms such as Facebook, Instagram, X, and LinkedIn. This format allows brands to use both organic and paid strategies to build engagement, foster relationships, and drive conversions.

- Organic social media: Brands can post content like photos, videos, and stories to engage followers without paid promotion. A fitness brand might share daily workout tips or motivational quotes to encourage its followers to adopt a healthier lifestyle. This is not only useful to the user, but it also generates attention for the brand. Organic content helps maintain an ongoing connection with audiences and can generate user engagement through likes, shares, and comments.
- Paid social media: Platforms like Facebook and Instagram offer paid options where advertisers can target audiences based on demographics, interests, and behavior. For instance, a fashion retailer might run a targeted Instagram campaign aimed at women aged 18 to 35 who show interest in clothing and accessories. This targeted approach ensures ads reach the most relevant audience, boosting the chances of conversions.

The Quest for the Self: Identity in the Digital World

Classical Greek philosophers were fascinated by the idea of the Self and identity. They dedicated a lot of time and effort to discern who we truly are and what our essence is when separated from the physical boundaries of the body.

For Socrates, self-identity was intimately tied to self-knowledge and moral introspection. Aristotle took a more practical approach, seeing humans as fundamentally rational and social beings. He believed that our identity is closely tied to our ability to reason, make ethical choices, and engage in social and political life. For Aristotle, "Who are we?" is answered through *eudaimonia*, or flourishing, a state of being which is achieved by realizing our potential and living virtuously.

An influential school of thought, the Stoics, went further in their definition of the Self; following the influences of earlier Greek thinkers, they identified identity as a product of inner virtue and resilience. For Stoics like Epictetus and Marcus Aurelius, we are not defined by our possessions, status, or even bodily health; instead, we are what our character and moral integrity say we are.

Plato's approach was on the nature of true identity reflected on the soul. In the dialogue *Phaedo*, he wrote:

> For we perceive that the soul is invisible, and that it goes to the invisible world—to the divine and immortal and rational; thither arriving, she is secure of bliss and is released from the error and folly of men, their fears and wild desires.

For him, the soul was something separate from the physical body, dwelling in a realm that is divine, rational, and immortal. This means that the human identity resided in the soul and was a stable, enduring part of us—something that survives beyond the mundane world.

The Digital Self

Now, think about your own identity. Up until 30 years ago, it was primarily defined by your physical presence and actions in the real world: who you were and how you acted. The people you knew and interacted with directly observed and evaluated your behavior and words, which, in turn, shaped your identity and reputation.

While there might have been a secondary layer of relationships (people who knew people who knew you) this network was generally limited. Celebrities, politicians, and those with public personas faced a different reality, their identities being largely determined by their fame. They often had to contend with public perceptions over which they had limited control. However, for the vast majority of us, this was not a significant concern. Our identities were largely shaped by our immediate, tangible interactions.

Fast forward to nowadays. We all maintain an alternative Self that resides in the digital sphere and is meticulously crafted and curated. Our usernames and passwords in each platform are as relevant as, let's say, a passport because they grant access to sets of services and resources. Social media platforms have become particularly dynamic arenas where our digital Self can flourish or falter. We now can build a reputation and even generate income solely through our online communication. Conversely, we can also face significant real-life consequences when things go awry. This may have sounded far-fetched in the early stages of the Internet revolution, but we have all seen sufficient examples of individuals losing their jobs or facing criminal charges due to missteps committed in the digital realm.

Our offline and online identities can be aligned or be dramatically different, but they have both substantial and share one important characteristic: They are defined by a set of identifiers.

To establish our identity in the physical world, we use offline identifiers (names, fingerprints, date of birth, and ID documents) as proof that we are who we claim to be, so we can access services (employment, health care, travel, etc.). Online, we depend on digital identifiers, unique data points or attributes that verify who we are, to recognize and track our online personas. They function as consistent, secure, and robust representations of our core identity in the constantly evolving digital landscape.

Plato's ideas on the Self and identity, particularly his notion of the soul and the ideal Forms, offer a surprisingly relevant framework for understanding digital identity in our modern world, especially in understanding how digital identifiers function.

1. Digital identifiers as core identity:
   Just as Plato considered the soul to be the core of our identity, our digital Self is defined by unique digital identifiers. User IDs, e-mail addresses, and biometric data like face or thumbprint IDs all represent a person's "digital soul" separated from their physical presence.

   In Plato's view, the soul is immutable and constant, it's what makes someone a person. Similarly, digital identity strives to create a "core" that remains consistent across various digital platforms; a stand-in for this idealized platonic essence.

2. Digital identifiers as reflections:

Plato's Theory of Forms declares that everything in the physical world is an imperfect reflection of an ideal, unchanging Form. Similarly, our digital representations (social media profiles, avatars, online behaviors) are fragmented reflections of our true selves. In different digital contexts, people display various facets of their identities; on a professional platform like LinkedIn, your profile and posts will be work-related, while on an Instagram account, you may share more personal views.

Just as physical objects are reflections of ideal Forms, digital profiles can be considered approximations of an ideal digital identity, each a "reflection" of a specific aspect of the user's core identity. The challenge in digital identity management lies in consolidating these fragmented identities into a unified whole.

3. Digital identifiers as authentic Forms:

For Plato, true wisdom derived from recollecting the Forms, an innate human knowledge which existed within the soul. Digital identity systems leverage some of these ideas and keep a latent recollection of credentials, login histories, and biometric data to verify identity. Each authentication moment can be viewed as a moment of recall where the system verifies that the user attempting to log in matches the original identity profile stored within its database. Where Plato's soul recollected the Forms, a digital system "remembers" the authentic identity and uses that recollection to determine if the current user is genuine.

Neo in The Matrix

The groundbreaking (for its time) film *The Matrix* (1999) offered a compelling, if somewhat exaggerated, depiction of the push and pull that people feel in the fragmentation of offline and online identities. The movie resonated with a generation grappling with the nascent digital age and, in dramatic fashion, foreshadowed the dissonance of identities many of us now experience with online services.

In *The Matrix*, our hero Thomas Anderson (Keanu Reeves) is a modest programmer who keeps an additional identity in the online world as Neo, the hacker. That is until he awakens from the machine-created virtual construct where he has been a prisoner. At that point, he again must reconcile two different identities, one as a real-world scruffy freedom fighter and another as a stylish superhero in an online simulation. Both identities are presented as equally authentic, each playing a role in the overarching story. In many aspects, *The Matrix* was just rehashing some of the ideas that Plato had put forward when he declared that every person strives for unity, integrity, and alignment with an ideal essence.

But at the time of the film release, the world was a very different place. Only 40 percent of people were connected to the Internet and spent just about 2 hours online each day, so Neo's identity dysmorphia was hard to relate to. Fast forward to the current day, where almost 70 percent of the world spends half of their days connected to some sort of digital environment or device and where managing multiple online identities across various platforms is no longer a fiction but a commonplace occurrence.

Just like, Neo, we all navigate a world where we present different versions of ourselves depending on the context. However, beneath those varied presentations, we share a fundamental desire for a reliable representation of our core identity, for a sense of consistency and authenticity in our online experiences.

The Key That Unlocks Marketing

The people behind the largest digital companies in the world want us to be connected.

If you own an Apple computer, an Apple phone and an Apple TV account, Apple wants to know who you are across those environments so they can better understand your interests and habits, what you like and what you don't. Similarly, Google is very keen on knowing what type of use people make of their search, maps, e-mail, and YouTube services at the individual level. The ability to use digital identifiers across services empowers companies to deliver personalized experiences that cater to the ever-evolving needs of their customer base. And by matching different identifiers across various digital environments, marketers can interact with users on any device they use.

Connecting those data points tells a cohesive story of the level of engagement a person has with the company. Applied to marketing, they can be used to generate revenue.

The identifiers most relevant for online marketing include the following.

1. Cookies:

   Cookies are small files stored on users' devices that help websites remember information about them. They come in different types, each serving a specific purpose:

   ○ By origin:
   - First-party cookies: Created by the website that a user is currently visiting. They enhance the user experience by remembering preferences, login information, language, location, and so on. Amazon uses first-party cookies in their browsers to remember what you like. If you add an item to the cart but close the session and leave the site without checking out, they will keep that product available in the cart for your next visit thanks to the cookie file.
   - Third-party cookies: Set by domains other than the one the user is visiting. Third-party cookies are commonly used to track user behavior across multiple websites for advertising purposes. If you visit a travel site like Expedia and search for flights, chances are you will start seeing ads for similar flights on other websites. This type of cookies was for years the most common form of persistent identifier online, but changes in privacy regulations and user perception mean they are being depreciated as an industry standard.

   ○ By duration:
   - Persistent cookies: Remain on the user's device for a set time period, allowing for long-term tracking. These cookies enable personalized recommendations over time. YouTube uses persistent cookies to remember your video preferences and history even after you close the browser.

- Session Cookies: Temporary cookies that are deleted once the user closes the browser. They are used for short-term tracking, such as keeping a user logged in during a single browsing session.

2. Mobile Advertising IDs:

Mobile Advertising IDs (MAIDs), such as Apple's Identifier for Advertisers (IDFA) and Google's Advertising ID (GAID), are unique identifiers that allow companies to track app usage and user behavior within mobile environments.

If you download a fitness app, later you may see advertisements for related products like protein shakes or gym equipment across various unrelated apps.

Apple's iOS 14.5 update introduced the App Tracking Transparency (ATT) framework, which requires apps to ask users' permission before accessing their IDFA. This change limited the tracking capabilities of MAIDs and was a response to both business strategies and increased privacy pressures.

3. Device Identifiers:

Device identifiers like the International Mobile Equipment Identity (IMEI) numbers, Media Access Control (MAC) addresses, and Android IDs are unique to each device, allowing marketers to identify users across apps and sessions on a single phone or tablet.

While MAIDs are unique, user-resettable identifiers created specifically for tracking in mobile advertising, device identifiers are hardware-specific ones assigned to each device. They are used for a range of purposes beyond advertising, including app security, user authentication, and device recognition within networks. Device identifiers are generally not resettable by the user, so they are more consistent over time compared to MAIDs.

A company like Uber relies on device IDs to deliver location-based promotions within the app so, if a user opens Uber at an airport, they might receive a promotion notice that is tailored for airport transfer services.

4. E-mail-Based Identifiers:

e-mails can be used as identifiers when registering for a service. Companies integrate these e-mail addresses into their CRM systems which allows them to connect a customer's online and offline interactions, thereby gaining a complete and unified understanding of the customer's journey. They can even add tracking pixels, tiny images that record if and when the e-mail was opened.

E-mail addresses, especially when hashed (encrypted in a unique, nonreversible way), are a reliable method to target users without exposing personal information. Facebook allows advertisers to upload their own hashed e-mail lists to target specific audiences. A fashion retailer with a list of registered customers can hash these e-mails and match them with corresponding Facebook user data to talk directly to them within the Facebook platform.

5. IP Address:

IP addresses are location identifiers that give companies a general idea of where a user is. IP addresses help with geo-targeting but don't uniquely identify users at the person level. If you access Netflix while traveling overseas and see a very different slate of movies and series, that is because the company is using IP addresses to tailor content recommendations based on the country or region you are in.

There are other sets of location data that are obtained from GPS on mobile devices rather than derived from IP addresses. But location data is sensitive, since it can provide companies with information about where you work or where you go in your free time, so most apps request user permission before they can access it.

6. Social Media Identifiers:

Platforms that control a closed environment with large numbers of users, like Facebook, Instagram, and X, create unique IDs for their users, enabling marketers to target ads based on what people do in that environment. These "walled gardens" have a full set of complex characteristics that we will look at in the next chapter.

Make Sure It Works: Measuring Your Marketing Efforts

For digital marketing, identifying and engaging a user is just half of the problem. You also have to be able to know if your efforts are being successful. One thing we mentioned regarding the Mad Men advertising era of broad media was how difficult they found it to know if their messages were landing. Digital media has solved the problem, so measuring the success of your engagement is a *sine qua non* condition for success.

Understanding marketing key metrics and performance indicators online is essential for measuring effectiveness and making data-driven decisions. These metrics help marketers gauge their reach and impact, ensuring that campaigns align with business goals and deliver a positive return on investment.

- Impressions are one of the most popular metrics to measure online engagement. They refer to the number of times an advertisement is displayed on a user's screen, whether the user interacts with it or not. This metric gives insight into the ad's reach and visibility. While impressions don't indicate engagement, they show the potential audience exposed to the ad.
- Click-Through rate (CTR) measures the percentage of users who click on an ad after seeing it. CTR is a valuable indicator of an ad's appeal; the higher it is, the more the ad content has resonated with users.
- Conversion rate is the percentage of users who complete a desired action (such as making a purchase, signing up for a newsletter, or filling out a form) after clicking on an ad. This metric is crucial for understanding how well an ad drives real business outcomes.
- Brand safety refers to the rate at which an ad appears in safe, appropriate contexts that align with brand values. Brand safety has become a priority because a brand's reputation can be damaged if placed alongside harmful or controversial content. Because of the large scale of inventory in online advertising, it can be difficult sometimes to verify every single page and app where the ad is displayed, so advertisers use tools and partnerships with platforms to maintain brand-safe environments.
- Invalid Traffic identifies fraudulent clicks and impressions generated by automated or malicious software (bots and malware). A high rate of invalid traffic skews metrics and can lead to

wasted ad spend if left unchecked, so advertisers use advanced algorithms and software to detect and filter out fraudulent interactions.

- Viewability measures the percentage of ads that are viewable to users out of the total ads served. For an ad to be considered viewable, at least 50 percent of the ad must be visible on the screen for at least one second (for image display ads) or two seconds (for video ads). This metric ensures that ads have a chance to make an impact, as nonviewable ads are unlikely to contribute to brand awareness or engagement.

A smart marketer will use all of these in conjunction to tweak and adjust not only the content of the message but also where it appears. High impressions with low CTR indicate a need for improved ad content, while low conversion rates with high CTR could mean the landing page needs optimization. Brand safety and invalid traffic detection help protect a brand's reputation and ensure ad budgets are invested wisely. Viewability serves as a quality control metric, ensuring ads are placed in visible spots for better impact.

It Is Art and Science but Also Sophia

Digital marketing is both an art and a science. It requires factual data points to make informed decisions, but, as Aristotle said in his rhetoric, it has an emotional component that is unquantifiable, intangible: it is the human connection that resonates with users. The best advice for companies looking to forge meaningful customer relationships is to, by all means, leverage everything that digital technology has to offer. This includes utilizing diverse online marketing formats, employing detailed measurement tools, and leveraging online identifiers. But the most crucial element is establishing a dialogue with customers that is characterized by honesty and provides genuine value.

Sophia is there to help guide the way:

- Plato's insights into the essence of truth compel marketers to pursue authenticity.

- Aristotle's rhetoric exemplifies the balance between *ethos*, *pathos*, and *logos* as critical elements to remind them that online connections should not be cynical.
- The Socratic method encourages marketers to engage in deep questioning and reflection to nurture an ongoing dialogue.

Applying some or all of these ideas will go a long way in improving your connection to your audience.

CHAPTER 7

A Digital Cosmology: The Walled Gardens

A Digital Cosmology

Imagine you are using a smartphone or tablet for the first time.

You have never been online and have no idea what the Internet is, but a helpful friend introduces you to the digital space and sets up everything you need for your new adventure. First, you use the search engine Chrome to browse through pages and pages of great content. If you want something more visually dynamic, YouTube has the solution with hours and hours of videos on every imaginable topic. After that, you may want to send messages to the new friends made online using Gmail, and before you head out for dinner, you can check the weather forecast in your browser and look for directions using Google Maps.

Now, since you are new to the digital world, this may seem like quite a complete online experience, one that touches many of the tools that platforms have at their users' disposal. But actually, all your newly discovered journey has taken place within a single environment; all those tools are part of the Google service suite. What you thought was the whole, full digital world was just a Walled Garden.

The term "digital walled gardens" refers to online ecosystems controlled by a single company which tightly manages everything that happens inside. Within these environments, every aspect of the user experience—services, access, user behavior and data, and monetization—functions seamlessly. However, a key characteristic is that data and user activity are largely confined within the ecosystem, with limited or no exportability.

Platforms like Meta, LinkedIn, and TikTok epitomize this concept. These ecosystems are characterized by their ability to capture and retain users, dictate their interactions, and create insular environments that discourage external reach. Most of our online time is spent not in an open blue digital ocean, but within a succession of isolated spheres intentionally configured to minimize interconnectivity. This strategic approach is not there by accident but by design because it allows these companies to maintain control over their users and the valuable data they generate.

Each walled garden is a universe, and to understand how they work, how they came to be and how they impact the user, nothing better than to look at the classical Greek concept of the cosmos.

Cosmos: The World As We Know It

The concept of *cosmos* (κόσμος), meaning "order," "arrangement," or "world," emerged as a foundational idea in ancient Greek thought. Philosophers of that time may have lacked knowledge of the Earth's geography, but they understood where Greece was in relation to other lands. The sky, however, was a source of wonder and curiosity. They looked at the stars, the sun, the moon, and the planets and pondered how it all worked. They wanted to unravel the mysteries of what they saw and understand the fundamental principles that governed its workings. Over time, their observations evolved from a general notion of order to a sophisticated metaphysical and cosmological framework that shaped how the Greeks understood the universe and humanity's place within it.

Homer, the author of the Iliad and the Odyssey, had used theological myths to describe the cosmos as the domain of gods before the birth of philosophy. The universe was portrayed as a hierarchical, divinely orchestrated order, with humans playing subordinate roles.

The idea of the cosmos as an ordered and self-sustaining system began with the pre-Socratic philosophers, who sought to explain the nature of the universe through reason and observation, rather than mythology. Heraclitus took a scientific approach and introduced the concept of *logos* (λόγος), as a rational principle underlying all of creation.

Pythagoras and his followers built on his approach and presented the universe as a harmonious system structured by numbers and mathematical principles. They believed it was ruled by proportions and ratios, with music and geometry offering insights into its divine order. It was Pythagoras who coined the term *cosmos* to describe the universe as a beautiful whole. The Pythagorean Cosmology saw the universe as a series of concentric spheres, with the Earth at its center.

Following these initial inquiries, both Plato and Aristotle further developed cosmological thought, albeit along distinct paths. They did share a fundamental premise: the cosmos existed as a self-contained, perfect, and inherently spherical entity, the sphere being regarded as the most perfect geometrical form.

Even early Christian thinkers were influenced by the notion of the Greek cosmos when it came to explaining the nature and structure of the world and Saint Augustine adapted Greek cosmology to fit monotheistic beliefs. He retained the idea of an ordered cosmos but attributed its creation and governance to a unique god, rather than impersonal natural principles.

In general, Greek thinkers, across various schools of thought, converged on a concept of the cosmos characterized by certain defining traits.

1. The cosmos is ordered and harmonized:
   The cosmos is a structured system, where every part has a place and purpose. While the specific divine or rational principles governing this order varied between different schools of thought, they all shared a notion of balance and stability.
2. The cosmos is interconnected:
   Every element of the cosmos, from celestial bodies to human beings, is interconnected. Changes in one part affected the whole.
3. The cosmos is self-sufficient:
   The cosmos is a complete and self-contained system, needing nothing external for its existence.
4. The cosmos is purposeful:
   The cosmos operates with purpose (*telos*), where every entity contributes to the greater good or order.
5. The cosmos is cyclical:
   Many Greek philosophers viewed the cosmos as an eternal ecosystem but one that renewed itself via cyclical patterns of creation, destruction, and renewal.

If you think about the time you spend on your favorite online platforms, you may find some of these traits are quite familiar. Google leverages its interconnectivity when it uses the data of your location via Google Maps, to inform you about the weather in your vicinity. Amazon maintains an ordered and harmonized environment where product recommendations, past purchases and subscriptions are seamlessly integrated. Meta often informs users of its different services on Facebook, Instagram, or WhatsApp of software updates and privacy policy changes in a constant cycle of renewal and upgrading.

Greek cosmology offers key insights into the world of the digital walled gardens, but before we look at those, it may be interesting to discuss why the walled gardens came to be in the first place.

All Under One Roof: The Rise and Traits of the Digital Walled Gardens

In the late 1990s and early 2000s, the Internet was a very different place characterized by its open nature. Websites operated independently, and users navigated freely between domains with search engines like Yahoo! and AltaVista. Monetization strategies were rudimentary, relying heavily on banner ads and subscription models. All in all, it was a slightly chaotic but free-range ecosystem—a place that, like the open frontiers of the American West, was seen by many as primed for systematic development.

This open model of the early Internet presented inherent limitations. User experience suffered from fragmentation, monetization opportunities were inconsistent and inefficient. Even basic data collection, the cornerstone characteristic of the digital space, was restricted. But more than anything, the absence of centralized platforms hindered businesses' ability to scale efficiently.

These limitations stemmed, in part, from the technological constraints of the time. Subsequent advancements acted as catalysts, driving changes in user behavior and creating new business opportunities. The rise of broadband first and, later, mobile Internet access enabled richer user experiences and platforms like YouTube and Facebook were quick to realize that they could deliver previously impractical services such as streaming video content and facilitating large-scale social networking.

The 2007 launch of the iPhone and the subsequent smartphone revolution further shifted user behavior, with mobile apps becoming the preferred method for accessing digital services. App hubs like the App Store and Google Play became crucial gatekeepers, granting their owner companies significant strategic advantages and enabling them to build closed ecosystems.

Arguably, the biggest impact in the digital sphere happened when AI-driven recommendation engines revamped user engagement. Platforms like TikTok and X leveraged machine learning to offer highly personalized content, creating addictive user experiences that boosted retention. Suddenly it was possible to keep users on a platform for hours.

Technology was not the only changing factor taking place. As the Internet and mobile digital devices became commonplace, users noticed the advantages of a digital-first life and gravitated toward environments that simplified their day-to-day activities. Why switch between platforms when Google's integration of search, e-mail, and cloud storage provided a seamless one-stop solution? The rise of social media platforms reflected the users' desire for connectivity and community, and they flocked to platforms like Facebook where people could speak easily with friends and family. It was not long before brands too realized they could use the social dimension of the platform to sell products.

Content consumption patterns evolved. Short-form videos, tweets, and posts; all contributed to our ongoing dependency on digital interaction. This shift represents a profound change in human behavior, arguably the most significant in centuries. If you think that is an exaggeration, think about the daily act of pulling a digital device out and checking the screen for updates. At the time of writing, you, myself and most of the people around us do this between 80 and 150 times a day.

A significantly negative evolution also has taken place. The initial dream of an open, civilized Internet, a utopian space for free exchange and connection, was tragically undermined by a growing sense of vulnerability and the honeymoon period of the digital frontier was short-lived. As fraudsters, scammers, and broadcasters of toxic content recognized the potential for exploiting the online realm, the idyllic vision crumbled. Junk mail, spam, deceptive friend requests, and the infamous "long-lost relative" inheritance scams became commonplace, breeding insecurity and eroding trust. The rise of trolls and the proliferation of harmful content added to the mix; civil discourse was increasingly difficult. Walled gardens, capitalizing on this widespread unease, emerged with promises of curated, secure, and "high-quality" experiences. They offered a haven from the chaos, implicitly acknowledging the failure of the open Internet to self-regulate and fostering a trade where user loyalty was exchanged for a perceived sense of safety and order.

Show Me the Money

The rise of walled gardens also had an economic component. The open Internet of the early days had a business model that left much to be desired. A good example was the publishing industry; caught up in the Internet hype of the early 2000s and out of fear of being left out, newspapers and magazines rushed to put their content online for free. They had no subscription or advertising model fit for the new digital space, so they could make no money out of it. Worse of all, they did not realize that the new channel would cannibalize their existing print business.

Meanwhile, platforms like Google and Facebook were the first to crack the money problem and revolutionized large-scale advertising by using user data to deliver hyper-targeted ads. This model proved highly lucrative, and advertisers achieved unprecedented levels of precision. Still today, Meta's Facebook Ads Manager offers tools for businesses to target users based on all types of precise characteristics, making it an indispensable tool for marketers.

Others, like LinkedIn, introduced "freemium" models, offering basic services for free while charging for premium features like advanced networking tools and insights. Similarly, YouTube realized that its ads disrupted the viewing experience and that some users would pay for a premium service with ad-free video flow and access to exclusive content.

All these monetization models work only if the platform has full control over the user journey and the flow of their data. A natural reaction from companies was, therefore, to close the gates and ensure the benefits of their services applied only as long as people decided to stay within their boundaries, the very space where data and attention are funneled into revenue. By offering integrated services, these platforms have successfully fostered user dependency, effectively locking users into their respective ecosystems. Yet another of the Faustian bargains of the digital world.

Gardens of High Walls

The list of platforms or ecosystems that can be considered walled gardens is long. We mentioned Meta, Google, TikTok, and LinkedIn, but what exactly makes a walled garden?

1. Centralized control:
   Digital walled gardens are marked by the centralization of power. The platform owner dictates the rules of engagement: what content is allowed, how data is collected, and how third-party entities can interact with the ecosystem. For instance, Apple's App Store and Google Play impose strict guidelines on app developers, while Meta controls what ads can run on its platforms. If the user wants to enjoy the benefit of the service, they have to abide by those rules or migrate, often losing their accumulated profile data (connections, post history, loyalty program benefits, etc.).
2. Closed ecosystems:
   These platforms limit interoperability with external systems. Google's YouTube prioritizes internal linking to keep users within its ecosystem, while Meta integrates Instagram, Facebook, and WhatsApp to discourage users from leaving its suite of applications.
3. Monetization via data:
   User data is the lifeblood of walled gardens. Platforms collect vast amounts of information to deliver targeted advertisements and personalized experiences. They have mastered the use of consumer data to gain insights (often around purchasing behaviors and interests) and engage attention. Google's vast corporate network is mainly financed via advertising revenue, a testament to the power of data monetization.
4. Network effects:
   Platforms need a "critical mass" of users to be successful, and walled gardens are good at leveraging network effects to grow exponentially. The more users a platform attracts, the more valuable it

becomes to others. LinkedIn users benefit from its professional networking capabilities while the platform grows as more professionals
join.

5. Algorithmic control:

The objective of every walled garden is to maximize the time users
spend within their environment, so algorithms are essential in curating content, personalizing user experiences, and driving engagement. Video and social media recommendation engines use AI to
serve highly addictive content.

6. Content moderation:

To maintain a curated experience, walled gardens enforce strict content policies. While platforms like YouTube avoid adult or mature
content, Meta invests heavily in AI-driven and human moderation
safeguards to manage its platforms' vast content ecosystem, ensuring user trust and compliance with global regulations.

7. Vertical integration:

In order to keep the user engaged, many digital walled gardens operate across multiple layers of the value chain. Google controls both
the Android operating system and the Google Play Store, creating a
vertically integrated ecosystem that enhances user retention.

Humanizing the Walled Gardens: Sophia in the Cosmos

In one of his dialogues, *Timaeus*, Plato describes the creation of the universe
as the work of a divine craftsman, the *demiurge*, who organizes the chaotic,
unformed matter of the universe into a harmonious and orderly cosmos.

The demiurge fashions the cosmos to reflect the eternal and perfect
realm of the Forms, creating a universe that is rational and purposeful. As
part of this creation, humans are given a unique role: they are not merely
passive inhabitants but active participants in its maintenance and understanding. According to Plato, human souls are created from the same materials as the World Soul (the cosmic essence that imbues the universe with life
and order). This connection gives humans a special responsibility: to live in
harmony with the cosmos by aligning their lives with its rational principles.

The human mind (*nous*), when cultivated through philosophy and
reason, allows individuals to glimpse the eternal truths of the universe.

In this way, humans act as microcosms themselves, reflecting order and purpose. That is how the Greek concept of the cosmos emphasizes humanity's role within a larger, ordered system: it is human perspective and interaction that imbue the environment with meaning.

In other words, the cosmos isn't just a collection of celestial bodies; it's a system that gains significance through human observation and interpretation.

There is a powerful learning here for the digital space of the walled gardens. For the last decade, the focus has been on the economic success of the different platforms and companies like Google, TikTok, and X have thrived. But, as Plato highlights, it is the user's actions within the walled gardens that give sense to these digital microcosmos. Users produce the data and the content; they are the engine that sustains the ecosystem.

Walled gardens are not a technological reality, they are a human one and have to be directed by a human-centric understanding. By drawing parallels between the ancient idea of a harmonious, interconnected universe and the closed, self-regulating nature of digital ecosystems, we can derive lessons for creating a more balanced and equitable digital future.

Order and Governance

Like the Greeks who saw order in the universe and tried to understand its laws, digital platforms need clear, ethical rules. User well-being shouldn't be an afterthought but a priority essential for their long-term success. Much like Heraclitus' *logos* governs the universe in nature, we need common rules (focused on fairness and responsibility) to govern all platforms rather than company-specific governance, which often prioritize profit over users. Platforms should focus on doing what's right, rather than short-term gains.

Interconnectedness and Ethical Responsibility

Digital platforms are connected within but also without, to the larger ecosystem and they affect everything they touch, from individuals to society and the economy. However, their self-interest often disrupts broader digital ecosystems, marginalizing smaller players and fostering inequality.

The Greeks saw the universe as interconnected, where everything matters. Platforms should see themselves as part of a larger digital world and act responsibly, like stewards of the digital commons, rather than as isolated entities. Just as the parts inside a platform are connected, they should connect and work with others, especially supporting smaller players. This is not simply a matter of good practice, but a fundamental principle for a sustainable digital landscape.

Order and Change

The Greeks grappled with the tension between change and stability. As we saw in the chapter about *panta rei*, Heraclitus considered constant flux as essential to cosmic harmony, while Pythagoras and Plato emphasized enduring patterns and eternal forms.

Same as the universe has core truths that act as a cohesive force, technology should adhere to the core principle of human experience and serve people. New technology should improve our lives, not force us to conform to technological imperatives.

Governance and the Common Good

The cosmos was an ordained natural system which ultimately resulted in the common good for the people. Digital walled gardens wield immense power over information, communication, and commerce, and their leaders must take an ethical approach, ensuring their ecosystems promote societal well-being. At a minimum, this means everyone should have fair access, be treated equally, and be protected from exploitation.

Purpose and Teleology

The Greeks viewed the cosmos as purposeful, with every element striving toward an ultimate end called *telos*. For Aristotle, understanding the purpose of a thing was key to understanding its place in the cosmos.

But platforms are commercial entities and while some corporate principles and declarations hint toward a higher end, they often lack a clear purpose beyond profit, leading to practices that undermine societal well-being.

Given their central position in the daily lives of their users, platforms should measure success by how much they help society progress, spread knowledge, and empower users. They should focus on improving the human experience, so people can thrive online like the Greek thinkers saw them flourishing within the cosmic order.

Sustainability and Eternal Cycles

No company is eternal, and no platform will be indefinitely relevant. The biggest gap when comparing the concept of cosmos with our modern walled gardens is that the former is perennial and the latter, perishable.

Platforms do have a way of ensuring relevance by improving in cycles: renewing themselves, learning from failure and adapting to new contexts. But improvement must be real; without forward momentum, the cycle becomes a self-perpetuating loop, rather than a genuine pathway to revitalization (Figure 7.1).

Gazing into the Future: Open Versus Closed

Walled gardens have two undeniable advantages compared to the open Internet; they offer an enhanced user experience and have designed a

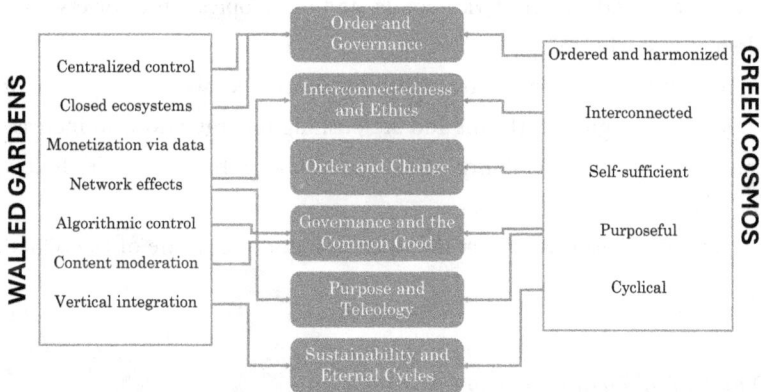

Figure 7.1 There is a strong parallelism between the classical Greek concept of the cosmos and the nature of the digital walled gardens as represented by these six principles

monetization system that keeps their services free or highly affordable while still making them profitable.

But they also face multiple challenges and criticisms. They may stifle competition and regulators in the United States and EU have caught up on this and accused them of monopolistic behavior, leading to multiple antitrust investigations and lawsuits. If you think about Meta's dominance in social media and messaging, you could argue that its decisions determine the direction and dynamics of the online sphere to a degree that is beyond the scope of any single company.

Digital platforms' pervasive data collection practices have ignited serious privacy concerns, highlighting the potential for audience manipulation. The Cambridge Analytica incident, in which Facebook user data was harvested without consent for political purposes, was a wake-up call for users and legislators about the tremendous power of the data that walled garden companies have access to.

But I would argue that one of the most significant and difficult-to-address challenges posed by walled gardens is their tendency to function as resonance chambers, reinforcing existing narratives or beliefs through the information and content they deliver. This results in a dangerously narrow and unidimensional information diet for users. The source of the issue is the reliance on AI-driven algorithms that constantly work to recommend "more of the same" to its users to gain their attention. This algorithmic echo chamber effect fosters the perpetuation of biases, the spread of misinformation and extremist viewpoints, and the suppression of diverse and alternative discourse.

Governments globally are rightfully concerned about the power of large, closed digital platforms and are pushing for regulations to increase transparency, interoperability, and ensure these global companies follow local laws.

So, how does this impact the open web and the future of the digital space?

The End of Dominance

The dominance of walled gardens has marginalized the open web, reducing diversity and innovation. While users flock to the large platforms, smaller ones struggle to compete for attention and ad revenue, leading to a less vibrant digital ecosystem. Although some innovative initiatives achieve global reach, the concentration of resources within a handful of companies makes introducing alternative services challenging.

Still, the future digital space may be heading into decentralization. Emerging technologies like blockchain promise to challenge the dominance of walled gardens by allowing users to own their data (via externally hosted ledgers), profile and connections outside the governance of global platforms. If we, as users, can migrate freely from one environment to another, the balance of power will change, and the walled gardens would then be just places where users choose to apply their information, rather than exclusive enablers and controllers of the process.

On the other hand, regulatory pressures are increasing and may force platforms to adopt more open standards. For example, messaging apps like WhatsApp could be required by law to enable cross-platform communication, reducing the lock-in effect.

At the heart of these considerations on technology, data and regulations lies the principle of user privacy and ownership. As people become more privacy-conscious, platforms will likely be forced to implement stricter data protection measures and, crucially, acknowledge the true property of the data generated within their walled gardens. LinkedIn, Google, Meta and the rest may provide the environment for user connections, often at great expense and effort, but it is the users themselves who cultivate those relationships and build their networks. Right now, they receive platform services in exchange, but this may not fully capture the true value of their contributions.

After all, a stage may be very important but not as much as the actors on it. The theater owners provide the venue, but it is the performers who create the experience.

An Ideal Cosmos

In the first episode of Carl Sagan's 1980 television series *Cosmos: A Personal Voyage*, the American astronomer said:

> *The cosmos is all that is or was or ever will be. Our feeblest contemplations of the Cosmos stir us; there is a tingling in the spine, a catch*

in the voice, a faint sensation, as if a distant memory, of falling from a height. We know we are approaching the greatest of mysteries.

Sagan was a scientist, and his show dealt with technical exploration and not philosophy. Still, there is an echo there of the same motivations that moved Greek thinkers to look up into the sky.

"The cosmos is all that there is," Sagan said and for decades, the walled gardens have felt just like that. They represent the culmination of technological innovation, user service and strategic business practices. And while they have created unparalleled convenience and value, they have also raised significant challenges related to competition, privacy, and diversity. Whether these ecosystems adapt to a more open and equitable model or continue to consolidate power will determine the next chapter in the evolution of the digital sphere.

The cosmological harmony, order, and purpose described by the ancient Greeks offer a crucial framework for evaluating contemporary digital platforms. They are required to reawaken human-centric principles and create a place where users are recognized not merely as data points but as essential contributors to their economy. By re-envisioning the relationship between companies and individuals, we can aspire to a connected digital cosmos that allows for innovation, empowerment, and a collective narrative that uplifts all participants.

CHAPTER 8

The Socratic Polis: Managing Organizational and Cultural Changes

Kodak and the *Polis*; Change Is Never Easy

John Kotter, a well-known expert on change management and a professor at Harvard Business School, analyzed what may be the most famous case of a company failing to transform digitally: Kodak.

In a 2013 article in *Forbes* magazine, Kotter wrote:

How can CEOs learn from Kodak's failure? Historically, Kodak was built on a culture of innovation and change. It's the type of culture that's full of passionate innovators, already naturally in tune to the urgency surrounding changes in the market and technology. It's these people—those excited about new ideas within your own organisation—who keep your company moving ahead instead of falling behind. One key to avoiding complacency is to ensure these innovators have a voice with enough volume to be heard (and listened to) at the top. It's these voices that can continue to keep a sense of urgency in your organisation. If they are given the power to lead, they will continue to innovate, help keep a culture of urgency and affect change.

As Kodak became more successful, complacency grew, leaders listened less to these voices, which made complacency grow some more. It can be a vicious cycle. It certainly was at Kodak. And if you don't address it first...good luck.

Kodak's case is intriguing because the demise of its film-based business model came at the hands of developments in digital photography, a technology that Kodak itself had invented. Steve Sasson, the Kodak engineer who created the first digital camera in 1975, received no corporate support for his idea. Instead, the company chose to run an in-depth analysis of the risk to their existing business by the new development and concluded they had a window of 10 years before digital became widespread enough to replace the film business. No further action took place.

Some tried to steer the ship. George Fisher, who served as CEO of Kodak from 1993 to 1999, attempted to lead the company into the digital age. Under his leadership, Kodak invested in digital imaging and looked to transition from its profitable but declining film business. However, the company's deeply rooted culture resisted Fisher's vision for digital innovation. Later, other executives like Daniel Carp and Antonio Pérez continued this effort, but the structural barriers within Kodak proved challenging. This failure to adapt ultimately led to Kodak's bankruptcy filing in 2012.

It is worth noting that Kodak's challenge was not about technology. While a technological shift certainly played a role, their failure stemmed from internal organizational and cultural issues.

George Fisher's case is not unique. Many other executives face internal resistance when implementing changes in their organizations, and this should not come as a surprise; human beings are creatures of habit and changes, especially substantial changes, do not come easy for us.

About 2,500 years before Fisher's struggles at Kodak, another man had encountered an entrenched resistance to change with much more dramatic consequences.

Socrates and the Gadfly of Athens

Socrates, as an Athenian citizen, was deeply committed to the idea of the *polis* or Greek city-state, a precursor of the modern country state that was central to ancient Greek civilization. The *polis* wasn't just a physical space; it represented a collective way of life, a political structure, and a shared identity that prioritized civic responsibility and communal goals over individual gain.

The *polis* emerged during the eighth century BC as rural communities transitioned from tribal and kinship-based organizations to more structured city-states. This shift was initially driven by population growth and economic development, but the Greeks realized a new social structure was needed as well, one that could balance individual freedom with collective responsibility, leading to the birth of the *polis* system.

The most notable *poleis* included Athens, Sparta, Corinth, and Thebes, each with unique characteristics but bound by the idea that all citizens (at least all free males) had a role in the political, social, and cultural life of the community.

Socrates, too, believed that a good life was inseparable from one's duty to the community and the group. He famously compared himself to a "gadfly" of Athens, continuously questioning and challenging the city and its authorities by posing upsetting questions.

The upper echelons of the city did not take kindly to this attitude and Socrates was targeted as a disruptive element. His teachings and influence were considered to have generated a nihilistic response in the youth of Athens; even worse, he was said to have supported the rise of an authoritarian oligarchy that challenged democratic rule. When he was put on trial for these charges, he defended his actions by saying that, although he may have been perceived as a thorn in the side of the Athenians, his questioning was ultimately for the benefit of the *polis*. He urged the city to value moral character and wisdom over wealth or power but was found guilty, nonetheless.

Socrates famously accepted his sentence and committed suicide by drinking hemlock after refusing exile. Who knows what the cantankerous old philosopher was thinking in those last days of his life, maybe he intended to send a final and powerful message: Criticism and challenging of the status quo are necessary and should not be stifled, no matter the price.

From the Agora to the Boardroom

The modern corporate organization may not be an ancient Greek *polis* but they share a core characteristic: both are collaborative environments where human initiatives are conceived, developed, and coordinated. The *polis* embodied the principle that individuals could realize their fullest potential within a collective framework, where personal ambitions harmonized with shared goals.

Consider a polis planning the dual challenge of securing its food supply for the coming year and preparing for a military campaign. Both undertakings demand high levels of collaboration, shared purpose, and alignment to succeed. The consequences of failure (starvation or military defeat) are dire. While a modern organization undergoing a digital transformation may not face such drastic outcomes, a failure to properly coordinate its human capital can still lead to its dissolution.

Some of the *polis* organizational principles translate well to contemporary organizations, especially those going through a period of change:

1. Shared vision and common goals:
   Citizens from the classic Greek period built the *polis* not just as an act of self-preservation but to establish a shared vision that is aspirational and acts as the "common good" to guide everyone's efforts. When employees in a modern organization understand how they contribute to the organization's larger goals, they are more likely to embrace changes and contribute meaningfully.
2. Collective responsibility and participation:
   In the *polis*, civic engagement was not optional; it was an expectation set for all citizens and, while it excluded large segments of society (slaves, women, in some cases laborers), it fostered a strong sense of belonging. In a modern organization that fosters participation, positive change is perceived as a shared responsibility, not just a top-down mandate from leadership. Empowering individuals, either *polis* citizens or company employees, results in a deeper sense of accountability and engagement.
3. Open communication and decision making:
   Regardless of size, most *poleis* would have their citizens gather in the agora to openly discuss civic matters. While for Athens or Syracuse, this meant as many as 60,000 citizens, others were much smaller, with between 1,000 and 2,000 recognized citizens. It is impractical for many modern companies to have open debates and decision making at that scale, but if there exist spaces for open communication and feedback where people can voice their concerns, the transformation process becomes a collective journey.
4. Unified culture:
   The *polis* was bound not just by physical space but by shared cultural norms and values; some were stagnant, and some were

dynamic, but they propelled the community forward. Most modern organizations have a similar cultural system in place, but that may just not be enough. It's having an embedded "culture of innovation" that helps employees understand not only *what* the change is but also *why* it matters.

The Wisdom of Change

Any organization is at risk of stagnation, particularly when it comes to fast-moving digital processes. And, as we saw in the case of Kodak, the challenge is more often than not the cultural shift needed to embrace the new technologies and working processes required to make it work. Blockbuster, Nokia, Yahoo, Sears, Borders...the list of companies that struggled to change their corporate mindset is long, but so is the number of companies like Domino's Pizza that succeeded.

Classical wisdom and Sophia offer key principles to help navigate these complexities to successfully transform. This chapter will explore five ideas and look at how they can be applied to drive positive change:

1. *Metanoia* (change of mind).
2. *Polymathy* (versatile knowledge).
3. *Agon* (constructive competition).
4. *Kratia* (good governance).
5. *Arete* (excellence).

Metanoia: *Change Is Not Just Good, It's a Necessity*

We spoke before about Heraclitus' *panta rei*, the concept that everything changes and that evolution has to be incorporated into our daily lives. Related to that principle is the idea of *metanoia*, which denotes a transformative change of mind, a shift in perspective that leads to new insights and growth. The Socratic method, with its relentless questioning, was designed to challenge assumptions and expose contradictions in one's thinking (leading to a state of *aporia*, as we discussed), but it also acted as a catalyst for *metanoia*.

A company looking to transform its culture has to encourage people to adopt new mindsets and let go of outdated practices. CEO and leaders who support *metanoia* have many levers they can pull to hurry the process along: change management workshops, employee involvement in transformation planning, upskilling training, and so on. Installing an innovation and growth mindset in the organization is what internalizes the need for transformation.

The key idea behind *metanoia* is enabling people to see change as a positive, ongoing journey rather than a threat; when this happens, resistance softens.

Polymathy: *Learn Everything, or at Least Be Curious*

Greek thinkers like Aristotle and Pythagoras valued *polymathy*, the idea of being knowledgeable across multiple disciplines, but it was probably Archimedes who best represents this principle. A true polymath, Archimedes excelled in mathematics, physics, engineering, and astronomy (and has gone down in legend as the inventor of an improbable "solar death ray").

Polymathy involves technical skill but also a precept of curiosity and discovery to expand the boundaries of knowledge a person possesses.

An organization looking to grow and develop must ensure that its employees benefit from a polymathic approach, where cross-disciplinary learning is promoted rather than discouraged. Digital transformation requires in-depth technical expertise but creating opportunities for employees to gain diverse skills in areas like data analysis, digital marketing, AI, and programming serves to both elevate the overall innovation literacy of the organization as well as to discover unexploited talent when new roles appear. A *polymathy* program that equips employees with versatile skills, making them more adaptable and effective in innovative roles, will fuel change and innovation.

Agon: *Compete to Improve, Not Just Win*

In the original Olympic Games of ancient Greece, winners were awarded olive wreaths, also known as *kotinos*. These were simple crowns made from the branches of the sacred olive tree in Olympia, symbolizing honor and victory. Despite the gruesome training and difficulty of the Olympic events, no material prizes were awarded, and the athletes competed for intangible rewards because Greek society valued competition as a way to drive improvement and excellence. The spirit of the original Olympic Games fits very accurately with the idea of *agon*, a sense of constructive competition or striving for excellence within a community.

While competition in the modern workplace can be ruthless, the principle of *agon* promotes an alternative, healthier culture of collaboration where teams challenge one another to innovate, perform, and adapt. As the organization's workforce develops its polymathic skills supported by a culture of transformation, constructive competition pushes teams to reach their potential, advancing its goals while fostering growth and creativity.

Kratia: *Leaders, Not Bosses*

While the Greek political system was far from perfect and authoritarian rule did occur, the idea of good governance, or *kratia*, was a recurring theme. It meant using authority in service to the common good, avoiding tyranny or arbitrary rule.

When reforming the city's laws to address social inequality, Athenian statesman Solon said, "I gave the people such laws as I deemed best, alike for the commoner and the noble, fairly weighing the right of each." And in Plato's ideal state, authority was to be exercised by a philosopher-king who, while concentrating authority, was expected to govern with wisdom and reason.

In an organization where innovation, upskilling, and constructive competition occur, the ripple effect travels upward and leaders respond by setting up governance structures that facilitate collaboration, accountability, and transparency. In the case of digital transformation, establishing governance frameworks helps ensure that data, security, and ethical considerations are consistently managed. Leaders act as stewards of the transformation, using authority not to impose change but to support and guide it.

Arete: *Extreme Ownership*

These different concepts coalesce in one of the capital virtues inherited from the classical Greek world: *Arete.*

Arete is the pursuit of excellence, not only on an individual level but as a societal standard. This concept has been present throughout history since the ancient world and examples can be found nowadays everywhere, from the meritocratic performance processes of professional sports teams to the demanding curriculum of Ivy League schools. Jocko Willink, a retired U.S. Navy SEAL officer, author, podcaster, and leadership consultant, reinvented the concept with his 2015 book, *Extreme Ownership*. Based on his military career experience, he outlines principles for discipline, leadership, and self-improvement based on the idea of excellence and *arete*.

In an organizational sense, *arete* feeds from the previous four principles and assures that the transformation process adheres to high standards of excellence across the company, driving everyone to contribute their best.

A Sophia-Powered Change Matrix

These five principles (*metanoia, polymathy, agon, kratia,* and *arete*) are interconnected and mutually reinforcing, operating across both the organization and its culture. A change matrix that integrates all five principles creates a continuous cycle of improvement:

- Management drives organizational change by embracing *metanoia*, recognizing the need for transformation, and guiding the digital innovation process.
- Employees enhance their skills through *polymathy*, acquiring practical and efficient knowledge. This upskilling fosters a culture of *agon* (constructive competition) as new opportunities and projects emerge, creating a meritocracy. This empowered and skilled workforce influences management, promoting *kratia* (good governance) and a leadership style that incorporates all members of the organization in the innovation process.
- Ultimately, these elements converge to create a companywide culture of *arete* (excellence). Both management and employees drive and hold each other accountable for continuous development (Figure 8.1).

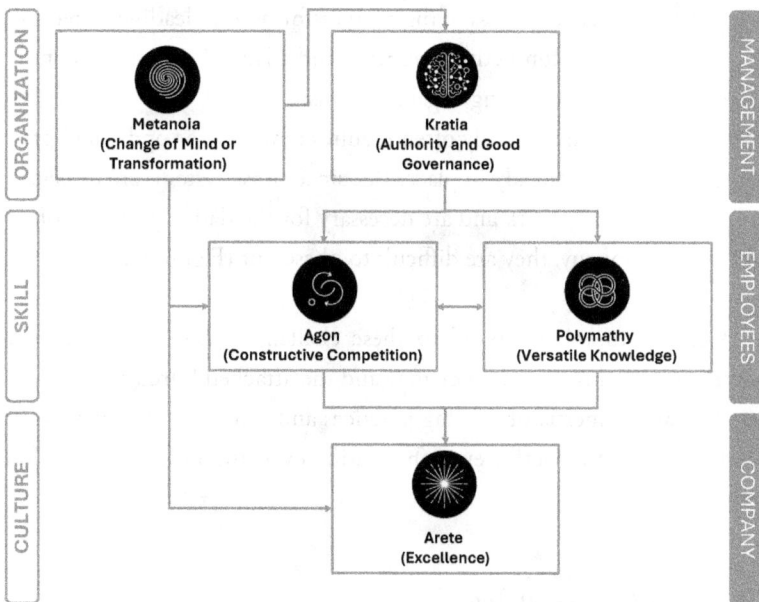

Figure 8.1 Classical Greek philosophy and Sophia offer five key principles to help navigate the complexities of the digital transformation process in an organization

Common Challenges: Changing Is Hard

Change is difficult. Disruptive change, the type that requires a restructuring of a significant part of the organization, is even harder.

It is not surprising that such different social groups like Kodak and the Athenian *polis* reacted similarly to the disruptive push that came their way: By clamping up and going into the defensive.

When a digital transformation process starts, there are three main challenges that a company may face:

- Resisting the change:
  Resistance to change is a common hurdle in digital transformation, as employees and leaders alike may feel uneasy about abandoning familiar processes and adopting new technologies.
- Fracturing into different groups within the group which creates a silo mentality: Silos, where departments or divisions operate independently without sharing information or resources, can severely

limit the effectiveness of digital transformation, leading to redundant efforts, conflicting priorities, and a lack of cohesive vision.
• Holding into existing, legacy systems:
Transforming digitally often requires removing or updating obsolete systems already in place. But since those systems are in place
because they work and are necessary for the daily operations of
the company, they are difficult to phase out (Figure 8.2).

Companies are not blind to these challenges. More often, they're
acutely aware of the need for change and the attached hurdles. The problem is that the inertia of existing practices and resistance to new ways of
working can be powerful enough to stifle even the boldest innovation
efforts.

GE Found It Difficult Too

These challenges aren't limited to small companies. Even giants like General Electric (GE) have faced significant blocks in their digital transformation efforts. Despite its vast resources and status as a quintessential
American industrial powerhouse, GE's early 2010s push to become a
"digital industrial organization," led by CEO Jeff Immelt, encountered
considerable resistance. The company's vision (to leverage software and
data analytics to enhance their traditional manufacturing operations) was

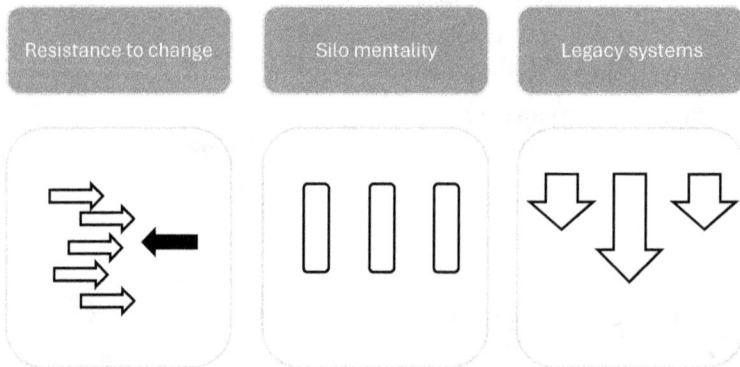

*Figure 8.2 When a digital transformation process starts, there are
three main challenges a company may face*

strong, and their industrial Internet platform called Predix had been de-signed to optimize industries like aviation, energy, and manufacturing through IoT and data-driven insights. The two of them combined held immense potential, and yet, the company still struggled to fully realize its digital ambitions.

The process started in 2011 when Immelt pushed the company to embrace new technologies and software capabilities. GE made substantial investments in software, including the creation of Predix in 2013. However, technology is only as good as the people who use it, and GE faced considerable internal resistance to this digital shift, particularly from employees in its more traditional manufacturing divisions. Many were accustomed to GE's legacy focus on industrial hardware and were reluctant to embrace software development and digital technologies. This pushback manifested itself in skepticism, and many voiced their doubts about whether the company's historical strengths could effectively be married with the new, data-driven strategy. Workers feared job losses and felt uncomfortable with the high-tech demands of the new processes.

So, what went wrong for GE? The company had a vision of where it wanted to go, it had a committed management team, a leader who understood the challenge and resources it could invest. But many of the issues that arose can be boiled down to the three areas of resistance we mentioned before:

1. Resistance to change:
   There was certainly a lack of digital fluency in the workforce at GE. The company invested heavily in training and talent acquisition by bringing over software engineers and data scientists, but it struggled to change the ingrained mindset within its manufacturing-focused culture. This resistance created a disconnect between the company's strategic goals and the actual execution on the ground.

   Over time, GE worked to improve its workforce engagement by developing training programs and by better communicating its vision. Immelt and his team pushed for a change in mindset, but the process was slow and met with mixed results. Although GE did eventually see some success with its digital offerings, particularly in its aviation and energy sectors, the full potential of the transformation was not quite realized.

2. Silo mentality:

GE also faced the challenge of silo mentality; its various departments operated independently, often leading to inefficiencies and a lack of coordination. GE's business units, including aviation, energy, and health care, were accustomed to working with their own specialized systems and processes. This siloed structure made it difficult for data to flow seamlessly across divisions. Each team had different business priorities, and efforts to integrate the digital tools across functions were hindered.

GE attempted to break down these silos by enabling different business units to share data and insights, which would in turn lead to more efficient operations and better decision. However, the lack of alignment and inconsistent buy-in from different departments led to delays in implementing these initiatives.

3. Legacy systems:

GE was very reliant on its legacy systems. Despite its bold vision for digital transformation, GE's core industrial operations were heavily dependent on existing IT structures developed over decades that had taken the company to the top of the manufacturing field. But they were not designed for the interconnected, data-heavy future that Immelt envisioned. For instance, GE's manufacturing and asset management systems were based on older technology that didn't easily integrate with the cloud-based services and IoT devices Predix was designed to support. The company's old systems were often unable to communicate effectively with newer technologies, causing inefficiencies across its industrial operations.

GE attempted to modernize, but the transition was slow and eventually decided to scale back its digital ambitions and reduce the investment in Predix.

By 2017, GE had poured over $5 billion into its digital transformation, including the development of the Predix tech stack and the acquisition of several software companies. By 2018, it was clear the return was not forthcoming, and the company was forced to roll back the program. The digital transformation had already fallen short of expectations and Immelt's successor, John Flannery, faced the difficult task of course-correcting. In 2019, GE announced that it would sell its GE Digital division, including the Predix platform, to focus more on its core industrial businesses.

It would be simplistic to say that the company's efforts were all in vain. GE may have failed to achieve its original vision, but it did incorporate digital capabilities into its business, and it learned more about its own manufacturing culture and its shortcomings.

Changing from Within: Kotter's Eight-Step Process

The challenges are there and no company, large or small, is immune to their effect. Fortunately, there are processes available that can help. John Kotter, the Harvard Business School scholar who analyzed the failure of Kodak, has studied in detail the transformation process of over a hundred companies. As a result, he developed an eight-step model for change management where, as described in his book *Leading Change* (1996), he offers an approach to achieving successful organizational transformation.

1. Establish a sense of urgency:

As a first step, companies need to understand why the organization must act by identifying pressing challenges or opportunities.

For example, a retail company may face declining foot traffic and growing competition from e-commerce platforms. Its leadership has data showing that over 50 percent of customers prefer online shopping, which makes it clear that without a robust digital platform, the company risks losing market share. Understanding this urgency would be the initial stage to drive change.

2. Build a leadership team:

Change must be driven in order to be adopted. Management is responsible for creating a powerful coalition of influential leaders from various departments to head the change effort. The team should be a cross-section of the organization, and include people at different seniority levels to give it a wider footprint.

A manufacturing firm looking to modernize can create a cross-functional "Digital Transformation Task Force" composed of IT leaders, production managers, and marketing heads under the aegis of the CEO. This team can act as an engine of change, collaborating to implement AI-driven analytics for supply chain optimization and ensuring alignment across departments.

3. Create a clear vision and strategy:

All change must aim toward an objective, and every company must change toward an improved new state. Developing a compelling vision for change and a practical roadmap for achieving it is a critical piece of the transformation process.

For instance, a bank can outline its vision to become the "most customer-centric digital bank in the region" and set a strategy that includes transitioning to cloud-based services, launching a mobile app with seamless customer experiences, and automating back-end processes for faster loan approvals. But it is the vision of "consumer centricity" that will vet what technologies and skillsets the company needs to bring to play. All those components must be there only if they serve the vision and if they have a role in the transformation process.

4. Communicate the vision effectively:

The best and most ambitious vision for a company goes to waste if nobody knows about it. Step four of the transformation process is making sure the vision is communicated at all levels of the organization. For this, management and the transformation team have to use clear, consistent messaging to ensure employees understand the end goal as well as the steps of the change process and its benefits.

A health care organization looking to roll out an electronic health records system can have its leadership communicate the vision for the company via webinars, by distributing newsletters, and by sharing success stories from similar health groups where the format improved patient care. Visuals and videos can help explain how the system will reduce paperwork and streamline patient data access.

5. Empower employees to act:

Change is particularly challenging if employees feel all decisions are being made without their input, so a key part of the transformation process is to remove obstacles and provide the tools and resources employees need to contribute to the change. The more members of the organization that actively buy into the process, the faster this will progress.

A global logistics company that upgrades its warehouse management system but encounters resistance from employees unfamiliar with the technology can address this by offering hands-on training programs, hiring tech-savvy coaches, and removing outdated hardware that slows system performance.

6. Achieve short-term wins:

The bigger a project is, the more important is to establish achievable, small-scale milestones that showcase progress. Focusing on manageable and visible successes early in the transformation process will build momentum and credibility.

If an airline company implements an AI-driven dynamic pricing tool for certain domestic routes as a pilot project, they can look at performance within the first three months. A demonstrable increase in revenue can be used as an argument to expand the tool to international routes.

7. Sustain the momentum:

Build on early successes by identifying and scaling additional opportunities for improvement.

After successfully launching a new e-commerce platform, a consumer goods company can shift its focus to integrating machine learning tools for personalized product recommendations. Then, ensure momentum by assigning leaders to these new initiatives and publicly recognizing teams for their ongoing contributions.

8. Embed changes in the culture:

Lastly, one of the most relevant steps is to change the company's culture. Integrate the new processes, behaviors, and systems into the organization's very core to ensure lasting change. Any shift that is not cemented into the company's culture and embraced by its employees is at risk of being rolled back

A telecommunications company that embeds its new digital-first approach by revising its performance metrics to reward employees who adopt digital tools, is changing its culture. Leadership can also incorporate discussions of digital transformation success stories into company meetings, fostering pride in the new way of working.

Challenges and Solutions. And Challenges Again

Kotter's eight steps are effective because they can be mapped very precisely to the three transformation challenges we discussed: resistance to change, silo mentality, and legacy systems (Figure 8.3).

But even with this roadmap to support your journey, things do not always go according to plan.

Sometimes, the resistance to change comes from external factors not fully under a company's control. Several years ago, a Japanese e-commerce company I met with was trying to implement a data-driven strategy. They

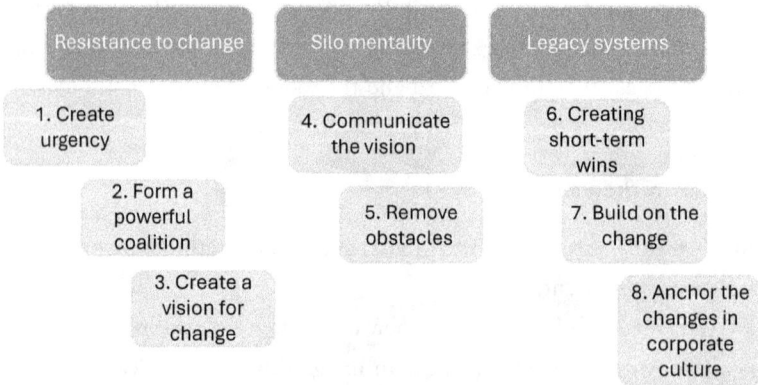

Resistance to change	Silo mentality	Legacy systems
1. Create urgency	4. Communicate the vision	6. Creating short-term wins
2. Form a powerful coalition	5. Remove obstacles	7. Build on the change
3. Create a vision for change		8. Anchor the changes in corporate culture

Figure 8.3 Kotter's 8 steps are effective because they can be mapped very precisely to these three transformation challenges: Resistance to change, silo mentality and legacy systems

worked in the retail space and, although they had no brick-and-mortar stores, they developed a well-built website where orders could be made easily; they also had an integrated payment system and a robust logistics process for order delivery. The company had done everything right; they were on point to embrace the digital age.

Then, orders started arriving by fax.

As it turns out, many of the company's products were classic fashion items aimed at an older audience. Its customers, mostly retirees in their 60s and 70s, would go online, select the clothes they liked, check sizes, and then, challenged by the difficulty of processing the purchase cart and completing payment, would dutifully fill in a sheet of paper and fax it to the company with their order.

The company did adapt to the challenge: It invested in buying multiple fax machines to keep its revenue flowing.

CHAPTER 9

The Ghost of Gorgias: Ethics in the Digital World

Gorgias, Facebook, and the Malleable Nature of Truth

When Gorgias of Leontini, a famed philosopher of the Sophist school and master of rhetoric, stepped up to the *stoa*, the theaterlike space where orators often addressed the Athenian public, he intended to conduct a thought experiment. Other citizens, including merchants, aspiring politicians, philosophers, and students, filled the area. They had come to see the polemic master debater at work. Some supporters wanted to marvel at Gorgias' skill, others wanted to challenge him, and still others sought to disparage him and his group of Sophists for their perceived moral flexibility and lack of ethical backbone.

Gorgias launched into his speech:

> *Men of Athens, you judge Helen as guilty—responsible for war, for death, for grief. But I stand here today to prove to you that Helen, daughter of Zeus, is blameless. I will show that she acted not by her own fault, but by forces beyond her control. And you will see that words—mere words—can have power greater than swords.*

The impact of this opening stunned the crowd. Gorgias was defending Helen of Troy, the most vilified woman in the Greek world. Murmurs rippled through the audience, hecklers complained loudly but Gorgias was not to be deterred. He went ahead.

Helen of Troy was an infamous figure in the Greek imaginary. According to the works of Homer, her (willing, according to legend) abduction by Paris led to the Trojan War, which caused immense destruction and loss of life. Helen was widely viewed as a symbol of betrayal, lust, and moral weakness, a woman responsible for the suffering of an entire civilization and the death of its heroes.

This was the subject that Gorgias chose for his famous speech *Encomium of Helen*, in which he argued that she should not be blamed for the war, using purely rhetorical arguments to absolve her of guilt. The speech was a test, and it aimed to demonstrate that, with skilled rhetoric, even the most despised actions or figures could be made to appear innocent or justified.

On that day at the Athenian *stoa*, Gorgias presented four arguments to defend Helen:

1. The will of the Gods:
   If Helen's actions were ordained by the gods, she could not be held responsible because divine will supersedes human control.
2. Force of abduction:
   If Helen was taken by force, she was a victim, not a culprit.
3. The power of love:
   If Helen left willingly out of love for Paris, it was because love is an irresistible force that overwhelms reason.
4. The power of words (*rhetoric*):
   If Helen was persuaded by Paris's words, it proved the power of speech to control and manipulate human behavior. Gorgias argued that speech is like a "drug," capable of bewitching and deceiving the mind.

Athens was shocked. Helen was widely condemned as a destroyer of families and nations, and defending her would have been unthinkable. Gorgias' ability to argue that she was innocent turned the moral narrative upside down. But beyond that, Gorgias' speech revealed how rhetoric could be used not to uncover truth but to distort it. By justifying Helen's actions, he exposed how vulnerable public opinion was to clever arguments, regardless of morality or facts. Gorgias' idea that words were like a "drug" highlighted a dangerous reality: A skilled message could manipulate citizens, judges, and leaders to achieve its ends.

None of this should have been a surprise. Gorgias was a Sophist, a member of a group of itinerant teachers known for their expertise in rhetoric, philosophy, and various other disciplines. Sophists were known for their pragmatic approach to real-world situations. They taught students how to argue effectively and persuasively, often for a fee, and challenged traditional beliefs and values, arguing that there is no objective truth and that all morality is relative.

This mercantile approach was not appreciated by many and received a strong response. Both Socrates and later Plato would criticize Gorgias and his Sophist school of thought for using words without regard for truth or ethics. Reviled by two of the most famous thinkers of their time, the whole movement gained a stained reputation. Plato went further and, in works like *Gorgias,* attacked the orator and compared his unethical rhetoric to flattery, a tool that pleases but does not enlighten.

But it seems clear that Gorgias made his point and in doing so, he sent a powerful warning: Knowledge that is not backed by an ethical framework can have negative and lasting effects.

Cambridge Analytica and Facebook

About 2,500 years later a little-known company called Cambridge Analytica came to prove how little ethical progress has been made in the quest to safeguard public opinion from the influence of manipulation. Similarly to the risk that Athens saw in the Sophist approach, this case exposed the risks of unchecked data collection, lack of transparency, and the failure of organizations to prioritize ethical considerations, often with far-reaching societal and political consequences.

In 2018, investigative journalists revealed that Cambridge Analytica, a political consulting firm, had improperly harvested data from up to 87 million Facebook users. The company acquired this data through a seemingly innocuous app called "This Is Your Digital Life," which tracked not only those who installed the app but also their unsuspecting connections. Cambridge Analytica used this information to develop psychographic profiles and deliver targeted political advertisements, most notably during the 2016 U.S. presidential election and the Brexit referendum, aimed to sway voters in a certain direction for its paying clients.

Overall literacy on how social networks used data was lower at that time, and the public opinion initially struggled to understand what the issue was. The scandal highlighted several ethical failures, among others:

- Lack of user consent:
  Users who installed the app were unaware of how their data would be used. Moreover, data from their connections was collected without any consent.
- Lack of transparency:
  Facebook failed to disclose the breach to affected users, eroding public trust. Cambridge Analytica started its data collection in 2014 and Facebook learned about it in 2015 without taking significant action until 2018, when news of the data harvesting broke in the media.
- Risk of manipulation:
  The data were weaponized to influence public opinion and manipulate voter behavior through microtargeted ads.

There was a significant failure of oversight on Facebook's part. The company had been so focused on expansion and revenue that its weak control mechanisms allowed third-party developers to exploit the platform. It had a tacit (and legal) commitment with its users to be the custodian of their data, but did not play its part.

The revelations triggered a global conversation about digital privacy, leading to widespread public distrust in tech platforms. Campaigns like *#DeleteFacebook* gained traction, with high-profile figures such as Elon Musk deactivating accounts to protest Facebook's unethical practices. Facebook faced congressional hearings, and its CEO Mark Zuckerberg publicly apologized for the breach. The platform implemented changes, including stricter app audits and user controls, but it was too little, too late; the damage had been done.

The case had a significant outcome: It catalyzed the implementation of data protection regulations. The General Data Protection Regulation (GDPR) in Europe, which came into effect in 2018, set new standards for transparency, consent, and accountability. Under its aegis, legislators can fine significant amounts to tech companies for noncompliance.

It's Not That Complicated, Really

The Cambridge Analytica case offers a few lessons, and if your company is working with user data, these are some of the key principles to keep in mind:

- Informed consent
  Collecting data without explicit user consent is unethical and often illegal. Users have the right to control how their information is utilized.
- Transparency is nonnegotiable
  Organizations must be clear about how they collect, store, and use data. Hidden practices erode trust and invite backlash.
- Accountability structures
  Businesses need robust oversight mechanisms to ensure compliance with ethical and legal standards. Failure to self-regulate can result in external enforcement and reputational damage.
- Ethical innovation
  Technological advancements should not come at the cost of ethical values. Organizations must integrate ethics into their product development and business strategies.

Gorgias's speech on Helen and the Cambridge Analytica case may be separated by a gulf of time and technology, but they are worryingly similar. Gorgias's thought experiment demonstrated that words alone could influence human behavior in ways that bypass logic and reason. And that is what Cambridge Analytica, using sophisticated technology and vast quantities of data, tried to replicate. Their experiment was to use data-driven targeted messaging to influence voters' emotions and perceptions.

For both the ancient demagog and the modern data manipulators, truth was a malleable concept. There is a sobering sense of continuity here: Some things, it seems, don't change that much.

Do the Right Thing: Best Practices and Digital Ethics

Digital innovation requires technology and an organizational revamp, yes, but at its heart lies the concept of data ministration. Many companies in the digital space have been remiss in maintaining such ethical considerations as consent, autonomy, and fairness when handling data. The truth is that having proper policies in place is both expensive and time-consuming, but it is also absolutely necessary. Often, the search for revenue or the drive to increase influence and gain consumer base means companies cut corners and take undue liberties with their users' information.

The current state of awareness around data is similar to that of environmental protection 30 or 40 years ago. In the past, manufacturing companies would dump their production waste without any consideration of the natural impact they had. As our understanding of the repercussions of these practices increased, so did accountability. In the 1990s, increased realization and stronger regulations meant companies moved beyond simply complying with environmental laws and began to adopt more proactive approaches to biosphere management. The change was costly; companies had to put in place new processes and tools for industrial waste management, and although it took time and not a few scandals, it was eventually accepted as a cost of business.

Similarly, it is taking some time, but most companies trading on data are more and more aligned with the idea that a strict management policy that prioritizes user protection is a sensible long-term strategy. When it comes to ethical policies in data and digital, doing the right thing pays off.

Still, one would not be blamed for thinking it is the Wild West out there. Out of the top 10 global technology companies, a surprising number of them have showcased bad data protection practices and even worse data usage ethics. TikTok, owned by Chinese company ByteDance, has faced scrutiny for collecting vast amounts of user data, leading to bans in countries like India. The app's data-sharing practices and potential ties to the Chinese government have raised concerns about national security and user privacy.

Others, like Apple, decided to lean toward self-regulation and a stricter approach. In 2021 Apple introduced App Tracking Transparency (ATT), which requires apps to obtain explicit user consent before tracking their activities across websites and apps. While Apple's CEO, Tim Cook, stated that privacy is a fundamental human right and emphasized building trust with consumers, it is not hard to see other corporate motives like a push to gain a competitive advantage (by limiting the ability of other companies to track users) and to strengthen Apple's brand image.

Four Things to Do

So, as digital transformation accelerates, businesses and governments have an ethical responsibility to embrace and apply best practices in their data management, but "ethics" seems quite an ambiguous term. What are the basic rules to follow?

Data Ethics: Always Obtain Consent:

At the heart of digital ethics lies the principle of respect for the user's autonomy and privacy. When we trust a company with our data, a value exchange takes place. We receive a personalized product or service, while the company leverages aggregated user data to enhance and capitalize on its offerings. For this exchange to be equitable, informed consent is essential. We have to understand, as individuals, what is the method of collection, storage, and utilization of our data and give explicit agreement. With this transparency in place, we can make informed decisions about whether the service's value justifies the data exchange. Transparency also mandates that companies provide clear, accessible explanations of data usage, rather than obscuring them within opaque terms of service agreements.

Apple's App Tracking Transparency (ATT), whatever its corporate motivation may be, means improved clarity for all users because applications must ask for explicit permission.

Amazon, on the other hand, has had issues around consent. The smart doorbell Ring devices, which incorporate video-recording capabilities, were praised for enhancing home security. But it was disclosed in 2019 that footage captured by these smart doorbells was shared with law enforcement agencies and third parties without explicit permission from users, sparking debates about surveillance, privacy violations, and misuse of personal data.

Regulatory Compliance: Always Stay Updated:

Legislation is often behind technology when it comes to codifying what is and is not permissible. The arrival of the mass-produced automobile was so transformative that it took years for cities and states to develop consistent regulations like traffic signals and driver's licenses. The emergence of commercial radio in the 1920s led to overcrowding of the airwaves and disputes over frequency assignments. Later, the rapid growth of the film industry in the 1910s and 1920s led to concerns over its moral influence, and it was not until the 1930s that self-regulation guides via the Hays Code came to be.

Digital technologies have gone through a similar legislative vacuum period but as public awareness over privacy increases, governments worldwide are implementing legal frameworks to regulate the industry. The General Data Protection Regulation in Europe (GDPR) and the California Consumer Privacy Act (CCPA) set strict rules on consent, transparency, and user rights while the Health Insurance Portability and Accountability Act (HIPAA) in the United States protects patient health data in the health care sector.

Companies need to understand the requirements of the legislation under which they operate and stay updated because the consequences can be dire. In 2023, Meta was fined €1.2 billion by Ireland's Data Protection Commission for transferring European users' data to the United States without adequate safeguards. The record-breaking fine highlighted the need for businesses, no matter how global their activity may be, to proactively align with regional laws to avoid financial and reputational damage.

In the brave new world of digital legislation, compliance is no longer optional.

Organizational Accountability: Always Have Internal Checks:

During my time working at Acxiom Corporation, a major data and technology company, I met Jennifer Barrett, who is often credited as one of the earliest chief privacy officers (CPOs) in the world and the first to hold the title at Acxiom. Her role was to oversee privacy policies and practices, ensuring compliance with data protection laws and addressing ethical concerns about data use in marketing and analytics.

This appointment, made by Acxiom in the early stages of the Internet economy boom, highlighted the growing importance of privacy in industries like data aggregation and marketing, which were increasingly scrutinized for their handling of personal information. It also sent a strong signal to the industry: Even if there are no laws in place, it is the company's responsibility to make sure that internal checks and balances exist to prevent consumer data from being mishandled.

Organizational accountability involves creating internal governance structures to ensure ethical practices. As in the case of Acxiom, this can take several forms:

- Regular audits to review data usage and algorithmic decisions.
- Appointing chief ethics officers or AI Ethics Committees to oversee compliance.
- Providing transparent reporting to stakeholders.

Trust as a Core Value: Always Prioritize Long-Term Trust over Short-Term Gains:

At the end of the day, users interact with companies and brands that they trust. You buy a certain type of car because you know it will be reliable, not just when you buy it, but after years of use. You travel with a certain airline because you know you will reach your destination with a certain level of service. When you use a map app to find your way, or a search engine to find information, you trust that the results are reliable.

Trust is built upon many small iterations between the user and the company, and any ethical lapses can break that trust even if the service itself has not changed.

In Summary

A company looking to set up its internal ethics and best practices framework would need to review the risks involved in poor data governance, the principles that need to be respected and, based on that analysis, determine the set of best practices it wants to abide by (Figure 9.1).

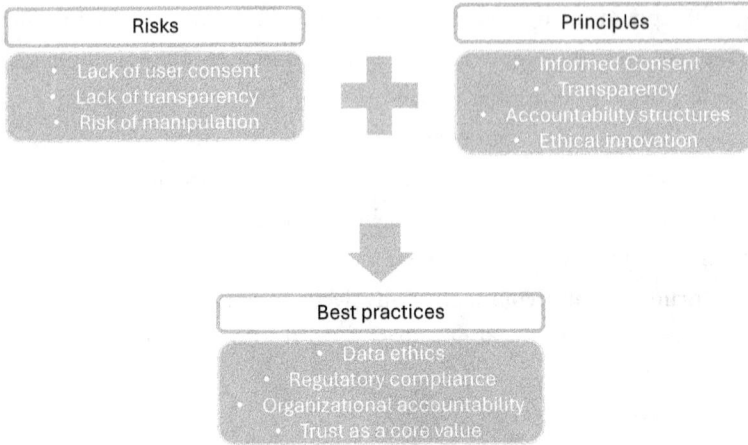

Figure 9.1 **A company looking to set up its internal ethics and best practices framework would need to review the risks involved in poor data governance, the principles that need to be respected and, based on that analysis, determine the set of best practices it wants to abide by**

A Very Fragmented World: Comparing Regulatory Models

Just like today's country-fragmented world, ancient Greece was not a monolithic entity. Different city-states had vastly different political systems and approaches to governance.

Athens had a democratic leaning (though citizenship was limited) with laws and regulations covering various aspects of life, from trade to public conduct. However, there was also a strong emphasis on civic participation and debate, so citizens had a direct say in lawmaking.

Sparta, on the other hand, was a militaristic and authoritarian system. Their society was highly regulated, focused on order and discipline, which partially stemmed from the large helot slave population that was the agrarian economic base of the army structure. Other city-states, like Corinth or Thebes, had their unique systems, often influenced by their specific geo-economic circumstances.

Together they shared enough cultural and social characteristics (particularly language and religion) to appear, in our eyes, a more or less coherent entity we call the ancient Greek world.

As digital technologies advance and the risks of data misuse increase, governments worldwide have adopted regulatory frameworks to address concerns surrounding privacy and ethics. But just as it happened in classical Greece, cultural and economic conventions shape the form these frameworks take. While there are shared goals, the approaches taken by different territories like the United States, Europe, and Asia differ significantly.

The United States puts a strong emphasis on free markets and limited government intervention, though this varies across sectors. Europe generally prefers a cooperative approach, with a focus on social welfare and environmental protection, leading to more comprehensive and stringent regulations. In Asia, regulatory models vary significantly. Some countries, like Japan and South Korea, have historically favored a more state-led approach. Others, like Singapore, emphasize efficiency and pragmatism in their regulations.

The United States: Market-Driven

The regulatory approach in the United States is largely sectoral and market-driven, meaning there is no single federal law governing data privacy. It has a more practical slant than in other areas of the world, perhaps influenced by the free-enterprising spirit of the country. The high economic value of its data-driven economy also means the purpose of the legislation is to instill confidence in digital activities. This includes increased security in e-commerce transactions and promotion of cost-saving online processes. Rather than having an all-encompassing data privacy law, regulation is industry-specific and includes a large number of self-regulation guides, industry codes of conduct and company best practices that are binding once the company subscribes to them. The Federal Trade Commission (FTC) is the enforcement agency for data protection issues and has the authority to impose hefty fines on companies in breach.

Key Regulations include HIPAA (Health Insurance Portability and Accountability Act) which protects the privacy and security of health data in the health care industry, COPPA (Children's Online Privacy Protection Act) regulates the collection of data from children under the age of 13 and

CCPA/CPRA (California Consumer Privacy Act and its update, CPRA) provides California residents with rights to access, delete, and opt out of the sale of their data.

The sector-specific approach allows for tailored regulations that address unique challenges in industries like health care, finance, and technology. But the lack of a comprehensive federal privacy law creates inconsistencies across states and industries, leading to gaps in consumer protection.

The United States' market-driven approach was evident during the 2018 Cambridge Analytica scandal. While the Federal Trade Commission (FTC) fined Facebook $5 billion, critics argued that the penalty was insufficient to deter future violations, showcasing the limitations of fragmented regulations.

Europe: The Gold Standard

Personal data privacy in Europe has an advanced starting point since it is considered a fundamental human right. Europe was an early adopter of data protection laws, back in the late 1970s, and has been consistent in updating them to keep up with changing technologies.

Europe's regulatory approach, exemplified by the General Data Protection Regulation (GDPR), is considered the gold standard for digital privacy and governance. Enacted in 2018, the GDPR applies to any organization processing the personal data of European Union (EU) residents, regardless of where the organization is based. This set of laws is backed by the Data Protection Commissioner, who is responsible for dispensing penalties to companies. Such penalties can climb up to as much as 4 percent of a company's revenue.

The key Features of GDPR align clearly with the ethical principles discussed before: Consent and transparency are required, but there is additional protection like the right to "access and erasure" (or "right to be forgotten") where individuals can access, correct, and request deletion of their data. Data portability rights give users the freedom to transfer their information between service providers.

However, these stringent requirements can burden small- and medium-sized enterprises (SMEs) that lack resources for compliance, slowing down the growth of companies and their global competition capabilities. Another issue is how enforcement across EU member states can sometimes be inconsistent.

The EU was not hesitant to take on one of the largest digital companies in the world. In 2014, a landmark case against Google in the European Court of Justice forced the company to delist search results containing outdated or irrelevant information about individuals, balancing privacy and public interest (the "right to be forgotten").

Asia: Diverse and Evolving

Due to the diversity of independent countries and the lack of a unifying political structure, there is no single legislative framework in the Asia Pacific area. While countries like Japan and South Korea adopt strict privacy laws similar to the GDPR, others prioritize economic growth and national security over individual privacy.

Japan's Act on the Protection of Personal Information (APPI) aligns closely with GDPR principles, promoting transparency, consent, and data protection. In fact, Japan's collaboration with the EU led to the world's first reciprocal adequacy agreement, allowing data transfers between regions without additional safeguards. And South Korea's Personal Information Protection Act (PIPA) is one of the strictest data privacy laws globally, imposing severe penalties for breaches.

In China, the Personal Information Protection Law (PIPL), enacted in 2021, resembles the GDPR but reflects China's focus on national security. Data localization requirements ensure that sensitive data remains within China's borders and privacy often takes a back seat to state interests, raising concerns about surveillance and citizen freedoms.

India, home to over 1.4 billion people, passed in 2023 its Digital Personal Data Protection Bill (DPDP). Inspired by GDPR, the bill aims to protect user data while enabling innovation. However, critics highlight concerns about exemptions for government surveillance and limited enforcement mechanisms (Figure 9.2).

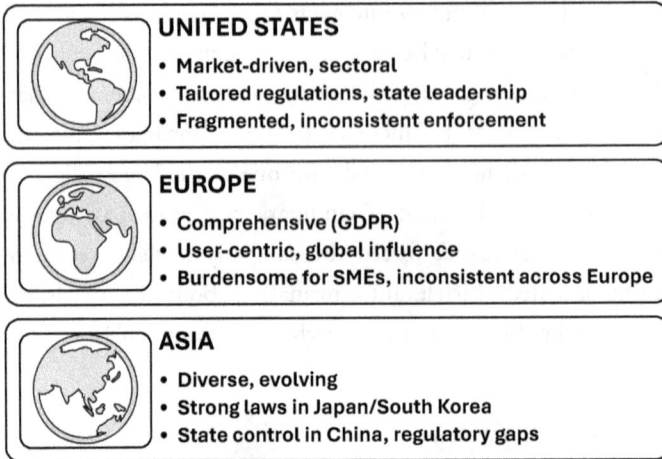

UNITED STATES
- Market-driven, sectoral
- Tailored regulations, state leadership
- Fragmented, inconsistent enforcement

EUROPE
- Comprehensive (GDPR)
- User-centric, global influence
- Burdensome for SMEs, inconsistent across Europe

ASIA
- Diverse, evolving
- Strong laws in Japan/South Korea
- State control in China, regulatory gaps

Figure 9.2 As digital technologies advance and the risks of data misuse increase, governments worldwide have adopted regulatory frameworks to address concerns surrounding privacy and ethics. While there are shared goals, the approaches taken by different territories like the United States, Europe, and Asia differ significantly

The Balance of Reality-Based Ethics

We don't live in an ideal world.

Very often, the realities of business and performance, especially in the digital space, mean there is a constant tension between persuasive rhetoric, technological advancement, and ethical responsibility, so there is a need to balance progress with accountability.

Ethics could be seen as a hurdle in the fast process of corporate growth and innovation that the digital sphere provides, but that would be the wrong way of looking at it. As long as there is room for manipulation, be it from demagogs like Gorgias or data companies with a vested interest, there needs to be a baseline of ethical considerations. Whether it's ensuring informed consent and transparency in data collection, maintaining up-to-date regulatory compliance, fostering organizational accountability through internal checks, or prioritizing long-term trust over fleeting gains, the core principles of ethical data handling remain paramount.

Ultimately, responsible data stewardship is not just a legal obligation but a fundamental component of building a sustainable and trustworthy digital future.

Conclusion

I remember walking out of a cinema in the autumn of 1999, after watching the movie *The Matrix*. It had come out internationally 6 months earlier, but due to Japan's convoluted release dates, we were probably the last country where it opened.

I was quite impressed with what I saw. Although a bit dated by modern standards (characters all dressed in black who wear their sunglasses indoors and sport names like "Dozer," "Cypher," and "Tank"), both the plot of the movie and the stylish editing were groundbreaking.

Most of us were still trying to make sense of the story and the central concept of a digital simulation, indistinguishable from the real world, where human beings lived. For me, there was a particular scene between resistance fighter turned traitor Cypher (the always great Joe Pantoliano) and Hugo Weaver's sneering Agent Smith that summarized the central premise better than any of the lengthy expositions done during the film by the hero's philosophical mentor, Morpheus.

> *[A fork stabs the cube of meat and we FOLLOW it UP TO the face of Cypher.]*
> **CYPHER:** You know, I know that this steak doesn't exist. I know when I put it in my mouth, the Matrix is telling my brain that it is juicy and delicious. After 9 years, do you know what I've realized?
> *[He shoves it in, eyes rolling up, savoring the tender beef melting in his mouth.]*
> **CYPHER:** Ignorance is bliss.
> *[Agent Smith watches him chew the steak loudly, smacking it between his teeth.]*
> **CYPHER:** Mmm so, so goddamn good.
> **AGENT SMITH:** Then we have a deal?
> **CYPHER:** I don't want to remember nothing. Nothing! You understand? And I want to be rich. Someone important. Like an actor. You can do that, right?
> **AGENT SMITH:** Whatever you want, Mr. Reagan.

I find it fascinating because of what it tells us about the nature of reality. Cypher knows the digital construct of the Matrix is just that, a construct, but after 9 years of living in a dreary post-apocalyptic world, he does not care. Reality is what his senses tell him is real.

Fast forward 25 years, and we all inhabit a digital simulation of our own making. It may not be as convincing as the Matrix, but it is potent enough to captivate, entertain, and disturb. We straddle two worlds, the tangible and the virtual, their realities intertwined. More often than not, we get confused and find it hard to define the blurred line between the two.

But I would argue that digital technology has not changed us at all.

It has changed the world, yes, but not our human nature. Not really.

All the anxieties that plague us, all the concerns we have developed about identity (who we are), belonging (how we fit in a group), and the world (what is reality and how we measure it) are not terribly different from the questions that have haunted humanity for millennia. We are merely grappling with them in a new, digital context.

The paradigm shift that the first Greek philosophers brought was systematizing the search for those answers. A search that took generations of thinkers on a never-ending journey toward enlightenment and wisdom. A search for an elusive objective, which they named "Sophia" and from which they took their name.

Socrates, Plato, Aristotle, and many others felt as insecure about the larger picture of mankind and the cosmos as we ourselves are, but they strove to find theories that could help us make sense of those great mysteries. The learnings they developed are out there, ready to be picked up, and, as sophisticated as we think we are, with our streaming services and iPhones and online influencers, our anxieties have not changed so much that we cannot learn from their lessons—from their Sophia.

A. Asensio. Tokyo, 2025

Glossary

Technology

AI (artificial intelligence): The simulation of human intelligence processes by machines, especially computer systems, which includes learning (acquiring data), reasoning (using rules to reach conclusions), and self-correction.

Algorithm: A set of rules or instructions that a computer follows to perform a task.

API (Application Programming Interface): A set of rules and specifications that software programs can follow to communicate with each other.

Big data: Extremely large datasets that can be analyzed computationally to reveal patterns, trends, and associations.

Blockchain: A distributed, decentralized, public ledger that is used to record transactions across many computers so that the record cannot be altered retroactively without the alteration of all subsequent blocks.

Cloud computing: The delivery of various services, such as storage, servers, and software, over the Internet, allowing for flexible resources and economies of scale.

CRM (customer relationship management): A technology for managing all of a company's relationships and interactions with customers and potential customers.

Data taxonomy: A structured classification system that organizes data into categories and subcategories to enable efficient analysis and retrieval.

Digital transformation: The process of reinventing business models through the integration of digital technologies, involving not only technology changes but also cultural shifts, organizational restructuring, and strategic planning.

Digitization: The conversion of information from a physical format to a digital one.

DMP (data management platform): A system that allows the collection and management of large quantities of data.

DSP (demand-side platform): A technology platform that allows advertisers to buy ad space programmatically across multiple media channels.

IoT (Internet of Things): A network of interconnected devices that collect and exchange data in real time, enhancing automation and decision making.

Machine learning (ML): A subset of artificial intelligence where algorithms learn from data to make predictions or decisions without explicit programming.

Metadata: Data that provides information about other data, such as its origin, format, or structure, often used to facilitate data discovery and management.

Persistent cookies: Small files stored on a user's device for a specified period that allow websites to remember information and preferences for a more personalized experience.

Programmatic advertising: An automated process that uses AI and real-time bidding to purchase digital ad space based on targeting criteria.

RTB (real-time bidding): A digital auction that happens in milliseconds to buy and sell ad impressions.

SEO (search engine optimization): Strategies to improve a website's ranking in search engine results, making it more visible to users.

SSP (supply-side platform): A technology platform used by publishers to manage and sell their digital ad inventory programmatically.

UI (user interface): The means by which a user interacts with a computer, website, or application.

User experience (UX): The overall experience of a person using a product such as a website or computer application, especially in terms of how easy or pleasing it is to use.

User journey: The path a user takes to achieve a specific goal on a digital platform or environment.

Marketing

Attribution: The process of identifying and assigning value to each touchpoint that contributes to a user's action, like a purchase.

Brand safety: Measures taken to prevent ads from appearing in inappropriate or harmful contexts, protecting a brand's reputation.

Conversion rate: The percentage of users who take a specific desired action, such as making a purchase, after interacting with marketing materials.

CTR (click-through rate): The ratio of users who click on an ad to the number of total users who view it, indicating engagement levels.

Customer persona: A semifictional representation of a target customer based on data and research, used to guide marketing strategies.

Freemium model: A pricing strategy where basic services are free, but users pay for premium features or functionality.

GDPR (General Data Protection Regulation): A regulation in EU law on data protection and privacy in the European Union and the European Economic Area.

Impressions: The number of times an advertisement or piece of content is displayed to users, regardless of their interaction.

Pathos (marketing context): An appeal to emotions in advertising to create a connection with the audience.

Personalization: Tailoring content, offers, or experiences to individual user preferences or behaviors.

Walled gardens: Digital ecosystems controlled by a single entity, like Google or Facebook, where data and interactions are confined within the platform.

Philosophy

Aporia: A state of puzzlement or intellectual impasse that initiates deeper questioning and self-reflection, central to Socratic dialogue.

Aristotle: A philosopher in classical Greece, a student of Plato, and a polymath known for his contributions to logic, metaphysics, ethics, politics, and more.

Arete: A classical Greek concept of excellence, both personal and societal, achieved through the fulfillment of one's purpose or potential.

Cosmos: In Greek philosophy, a harmonious and ordered universe governed by rational principles, often considered in relation to human purpose.

Ethos: A rhetorical appeal to credibility or character, used to persuade an audience.

Epicurus: A Greek philosopher and founder of Epicureanism, a philosophy that emphasized maximizing pleasure and minimizing pain, while advocating for a simple and virtuous life.

Gorgias: A Greek sophist known for his skeptical philosophy and his views on rhetoric as a powerful tool of persuasion, regardless of truth.

Heraclitus: A pre-Socratic Greek philosopher known for his doctrine of change, famously stating, "No man ever steps in the same river twice."

Logos: A rhetorical appeal to logic and reason, often underpinned by evidence and structured argumentation.

Metanoia: A transformative change in one's way of thinking, often leading to growth and new understanding.

Pathos: In rhetoric, an emotional appeal designed to persuade or move the audience by eliciting feelings.

Philosophy: A discipline of thought originated in classical Greece. From the ancient Greek word Sophia, it means "Love of Wisdom."

Plato: A philosopher in classical Greece, a student of Socrates, and the founder of the Academy in Athens, the first institution of higher learning in the Western world.

Polis: A term for a city-state in ancient Greece. It represented the center of Greek social and political life.

Phronesis: Practical wisdom that involves making sound judgments in real-life situations, emphasized in Aristotle's ethics.

Rhetoric: The art of effective or persuasive speaking or writing, a concept developed and studied extensively by Aristotle.

Sophia: The Greek concept of wisdom that combines practical knowledge, moral insight, and intellectual understanding.

Socrates: A Greek philosopher from Athens who is widely credited as the father of Western philosophy and the Socratic method, a form of inquiry and debate based on asking questions to stimulate critical thinking and illuminate ideas.

Telos: A term referring to the purpose or ultimate aim of an entity or action, central to Aristotelian philosophy.

Bibliography

Asensio, Alfonso. *World Wide Data: The Future of Digital Marketing, E-Commerce, and Big Data*. Business Expert Press, 2017.

Aristotle. *On Rhetoric: A Theory of Civic Discourse*. Translated by George A. Kennedy. Oxford University Press, 1991.

Herodotus. *The Histories. The Landmark Herodotus*, edited by Robert B. Strassler. Pantheon, 2007.

Homer. *The Iliad*. Translated by Robert Fagles. Penguin Books, 1990.

Homer. *The Odyssey*. Translated by Robert Fagles. Penguin Books, 1996.

Luther, Martin. *The Ninety-Five Theses and Other Writings*. Translated by William R. Russell. Penguin Classics, 2017.

Messner-Loebs, William (writer) and Kieth, Sam (art). *Epicurus the Sage*. WildStorm/Cliffhanger (collected edition), 2003.

Plato. *Meno*. Translated by W. K. C. Guthrie. Cambridge University Press, 1961.

Plato. *Republic*. Translated by H.D.P. Lee. Penguin Classics, 1955.

About the Author

Alfonso Asensio is a Tokyo-based executive at a leading global digital technology company, who specializes in data-driven marketing and digital transformation. Alfonso is a trilingual professional with a digital marketing certification from the University of California, Berkeley, and a master's degree from Nagoya University in Japan. His professional background includes business roles at major Japanese consumer corporations and Silicon Valley tech firms.

Alfonso has lectured at Rikkyo University and Hitotsubashi University in Tokyo, and he is a lecturer in digital transformation at Temple University.

Digital Wisdom is his third book, after *World Wide Data: The Future of Digital Marketing, E-Commerce, and Big Data* (2018) and *Chief Kickboxing Officer: Applying the Fight Mentality to Business Success* (2019), both published by Business Expert Press (New York).

Index

www.ingramcontent.com/pod-product-compliance
Lightning Source LLC
Chambersburg PA
CBHW061305220326
41599CB00026B/4739